ENRICHMENT CLUSTERS

SECOND EDITION

ENRICHMENT CLUSTERS

a practical plan for real-world, student-driven learning

Joseph S. Renzulli,
Marcia Gentry,
and Sally M. Reis

PRUFROCK PRESS INC.
WACO, TEXAS

ACKNOWLEDGEMENTS

This book is in honor of our mothers, Letitia Morgan and Jacky Gentry, and the many creative and dedicated teachers throughout the United States who participated in the enrichment cluster studies.

Special thanks go to Arnold Gamboa, Jason McIntosh, Kristina Ayers Paul, and Jeff Spanke for their insights and suggestions.

Prufrock Press Inc.
P.O. Box 8813
Waco, TX 76714-8813
Phone: (800) 998-2208
Fax: (800) 240-0333
http://www.prufrock.com

TABLE OF CONTENTS

ACKNOWLEDGEMENTS v

CHAPTER 1   Freedom to Teach... 1
CHAPTER 2   What Is an Enrichment Cluster?.. 17
CHAPTER 3   Seven Steps to Implementing an Enrichment Cluster Program..... 37
CHAPTER 4   How to Develop Your Own Enrichment Cluster....................... 61
CHAPTER 5   Staff Development and Program Evaluation 85
CHAPTER 6   Research Underlying the Enrichment Cluster Program............ 151

REFERENCES 163

APPENDIX A   If I Ran the School Survey 165
APPENDIX B   Sample Enrichment Cluster Descriptions 169
APPENDIX C   Methodological Resources...................................... 177

ABOUT THE AUTHORS 189
INDEX 191

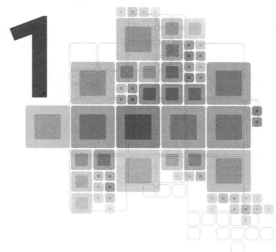

FREEDOM TO TEACH

Suddenly I remembered why I had gone into teaching in the first place. I had forgotten, and I didn't even know I had forgotten. Then I remembered what I had always thought teaching would be all about.
—Middle School Teacher in the
Enrichment Cluster Research Project

Most teachers have had, at some point, a vision about what they thought teaching would be all about. They pictured themselves in classrooms with interested and excited students listening in rapt attention to fascinating tales about dangerous midnight movements on the Underground Railroad. They imagined young people happily gathered around a science table to discover the mysteries of how things work, or experiencing an "Ah-ha!" moment when the relationships between a set of numbers start to make sense. They saw in their mind's eye a child's joy when hearing praise for a creative story or science project, eager to work on suggestions to make it even better. Some prospective teachers even fantasized about the e-mail or phone call from a former student saying that a play she wrote was going into production, and it all started when she was a student in the teacher's creative writing class so many years ago.

For many teachers, there is a stark disconnect between their vision of a challenging and rewarding career and the day-to-day grind of the profession. Perhaps most ironic about the difference between the ideal and the reality of today's classrooms is that most teachers have the skills and motivation to do the kinds of teaching about which they once dreamed. Unfortunately, the regulations and requirements imposed upon them "from above" have resulted in both a prescriptive approach to teaching and a barrier to creating a challenging and exciting classroom. Overprescribing the work of teachers has, in some cases, lobotomized good teachers and denied them the creative teaching opportunities that attracted them to the profession in the first place. Linda Darling-Hammond (1997) reported that most teachers felt that their views of good teaching were at odds with those of their school districts. Seventy-nine percent of the teachers participating in this study indicated that concerns for children and for learning are central to good teaching, but only 11% said that their school district shared this view. A large majority of teachers (75%) believed that their school officials favored behaviorist theories of learning rather than theories that are more child-centered and constructivist. With the focus shifting to teacher accountability in recent years, frequently using measures that do not indicate quality teaching or quality teachers (Darling-Hammond, 2009), this tension has undoubtedly increased. In fact, 50% of teachers now leave the profession within their first 5 years of teaching (Ingersoll & Perda, 2010), a frightening statistic in a time when good, committed teachers are needed more than ever. Diane Ravitch (2010) pointed out that reform efforts, with their concentration on test scores and punitive accountability, are ruining America's public schools for students and for their teachers.

This book provides a rationale and a practical set of guidelines for a program that supports a different brand of learning from the approach that guides activities in many classrooms today. We call this brand *student-driven learning*, and the vehicles designed to deliver this more creative pedagogical method are enrichment clusters. Enrichment clusters are student centered—directed by student interest and the development of authentic products for real audiences—and based on both common sense and research challenging the assertion that important intellectual growth can only be charted through an information transfer and standardized testing approach to education (Gentry, Reis, & Moran, 1999; Reis & Gentry, 1998).

We do not think that all prescribed, textbook-driven, standards-based teaching is bad, nor do we criticize the current national movement to improve the achievement of our nation's young people. But we do believe that a good education should balance a prescribed curriculum with regular, systematic opportunities for students to develop their abilities, interests, and learning strengths. This balance must be achieved in an atmosphere that places a premium on enjoyment and collaboration and allows students to engage in investigative activities with high levels of creative productivity. Even within the current trend toward an externally determined, "top-down" curriculum, teachers must have some opportunities to teach in a manner that is more consistent with the ideals that attracted them to the profession. As one teacher put it, "I am tired of being the administrator of a textbook and the victim of a system that fails to recognize my talents and creativity. Enrichment clusters gave me the opportunity to do some real teaching."

The main purpose of developing an enrichment cluster program is to create a time and a place within the school week for student-driven learning to be on the front burner of student and teacher activity. Although we would like to see more of this type of learning infused into the overall curriculum, the external forces that dominate most schools are simply too powerful to allow for massive immediate change. Educational change seldom takes place at the center of things; instead, it evolves on the fringes where dedicated people exercise their judgment in the best interest of the young people for whom they are responsible. And successful change occurring on the edges has been found to seep toward the center. In the research we conducted on enrichment clusters (see Chapter 6: Research Underlying the Enrichment Cluster Program), we found that many of the strategies teachers used to facilitate enrichment clusters found their way into everyday teaching practices in regular classrooms. Through strategies such as creative compliance and the infiltrator model of school change, we have witnessed remarkable changes taking place in mainstream classrooms.

WHY STUDENT-DRIVEN LEARNING IS IMPORTANT FOR OUR SCHOOLS AND THE NATION

Student-driven learning is based on an inductive approach that provides students with opportunities to apply and extend the basic knowledge and skills that are the legitimate outcomes of a deductive learning model. Our aim is not to do away with deductive learning, but instead, to achieve balance between deductive and inductive learning. Deductive learning is the process of reaching predetermined conclusions by applying general rules to a problem. It is similar in nature to what is frequently referred to as *convergent thinking*—focusing or "converging" on the correct answer. Inductive thinking is the process of reaching a conclusion by gathering data, categorizing and interpreting it, and drawing conclusions based on the data rather than a set of rules. It is similar to divergent thinking and the process of creativity.

Introducing inductive learning into the school is important for several reasons. First, schools should be enjoyable places that students want to attend rather than places they endure as part of their journey toward assimilation into the job market and the adult world. Second, schools should be places where students participate and prepare for intelligent, creative, and effective living. This type of living demands the ability to analyze, criticize, and select from alternative sources of information and courses of action; to think effectively about unpredictable personal and interpersonal problems; to live harmoniously with others while remaining true to an emerging personal system of attitudes, beliefs, and values; and to confront, clarify, and act upon problems and situations in constructive and creative ways.

All of America knows that there are two school systems in our nation. One school system—the one that serves poor and mainly minority students—has generally failed to make the kind of progress that leads to high achievement, matriculation into higher education, and improved standards of living. Billions of dollars and massive reform efforts aimed at addressing the problem of poor schools have focused largely on compensatory and remedial models. Most would agree that the positive results of these school reform efforts have ranged from minimal to nonexistent. By contrast, America's other school system—the one that serves mainly middle-class White students—has been successful enough to produce one of the most affluent and productive societies in the history of the world.

Endless state regulations and pressures to "get the scores up" have caused both school systems to buy into using more and more highly prescriptive models of teaching. As a result, schools continue to withhold high-level learning opportunities from poor children, and they are now slowly dismantling those aspects of our successful schools that have contributed to our nation's inventiveness, entrepreneurship, and creative productivity.

Student-driven learning is important because our society's economic and cultural growth, and even our democratic way of life, depend on an unlimited reservoir of creative and effective people. One idea for a new product, or the start of a new business, has the potential to create millions of jobs or cultural enrichments that contribute to a better way of life for many Americans. A small number of individuals will emerge as creative thinkers and problem solvers, but we as a society cannot afford to leave the emergence of such leaders to chance, nor can we continue to lose the undeveloped talents of so many of our young citizens to poverty. All students must have opportunities to develop their unique talents and potentials and to lead constructive lives. We have no argument with the importance of basic skill learning, but without an equal investment in the teaching and learning that promotes talent development, leadership, and creative productivity, our schools will devolve.

LEARNING THEORY 101:
THE SHORT COURSE

Every teacher remembers taking a course in educational psychology in which he or she devoted time to various theories of learning. Whether someone remembers and implements these theories once he or she becomes a teacher is another matter. But a couple of ideas about learning from those courses are actually very relevant, and we will focus on those few points. (Readers interested in a more detailed discussion of the theory underlying the brand of learning upon which

	Learning Theory	
	Deductive	**Inductive**
Pedagogy	Deductive Didactic & Prescriptive Knowledge, Acquisition, Storage, and Retrieval. Predetermined Content	Inductive, Investigative, & Inquiry Oriented Knowledge Application, High Engagement, Motivation, and Enjoyment J-I-T Content
Outcomes	Basic Skill Acquisition Text Consumption	21st Century Thinking Skills Creative Productivity
Major Theorists	Behaviorists • Pavlov • Thorndike • Skinner	Constructivists • Pestalozzi, Torrance • Montessori, Gardner • Piaget & Bruner • Dewey, Steinberg
National Goals	Increased Academic Achievement Higher Test Scores Technically Proficient Professional and Skilled Workers	Inventors Creative Designers in Sciences, Arts, & Technology Innovative Leaders Entrepreneurs Writers People Who Make a Difference

FIGURE 1.1. Continuum of Learning Theories

enrichment clusters are based can refer to "The Definition of High-End Learning" at http://www.gifted.uconn.edu/sem/semart10.html).

First, it is important to remember that all learning exists on a continuum ranging from deductive or didactic approaches at one end to inductive or constructive approaches at the other (see Figure 1.1). This continuum exists for learners of all ages—from toddlers to doctoral students—and in all areas of curricular activity. The continuum also exists for learning that takes place in the nonschool world, the kind that young people and adults pursue as they go about acquiring new skills for their jobs or working in the kitchen, the garden, or the workshop in the basement. Both models of learning and teaching are valuable in the overall process of schooling, and a well-balanced school program must make use of basic and high-end approaches as well as the combined approaches between the two ends of the continuum.

THE DEDUCTIVE MODEL OF LEARNING

Although many names have been used to describe the theories that define the ends of the learning continuum, we simply refer to them as the deductive model and the inductive model. The deductive model is familiar to most educators and guides most of what takes place in classrooms and other places of formal learning.

The inductive model, on the other hand, represents the kind of learning that typically takes place outside formal school situations. Classrooms are characterized by fixed time schedules, segmented subjects or topics, predetermined sets of information and activities, tests and grades to determine progress, and a pattern of organization largely driven by the need to acquire information and skills that are deemed important by curriculum developers, textbook publishers, and committees that prepare lists of standards. The deductive model assumes that current learning will have transfer value for some future problem, course, occupational pursuit, or life activity.

Deductive learning is based mainly on the factory model or human engineering conception of schooling. The underlying psychological theory is behaviorism, and the theorists most associated with this model are Ivan Pavlov, E. L. Thorndike, and B. F. Skinner. This ideology centers on the ability to produce desired responses by presenting selected stimuli. In an educational setting, the theory translates into a form of structured training for purposes of knowledge and skill acquisition. A curriculum based on the deductive model must be examined in terms of both what and how something is taught. The issue of what is (or should be) taught has always been the subject of controversy, ranging from a conservative position that emphasizes a classical or basic education curriculum to a more liberal perspective that includes contemporary knowledge and life adjustment experiences (e.g., driver's education, sex education, computer literacy). Overall, American schools have been very effective in adapting what is taught to changes taking place in society. Recent concerns about the kinds of skills that a rapidly changing job market will require have accelerated curricular changes that prepare students for careers in technological fields and a postindustrial society. Nowhere is this change more evident than in the emphasis currently placed on thinking skills, interdisciplinary approaches to curriculum, and the use of technology in the learning process. These changes are favorable developments, but the deductive model still limits learning because it restricts both what is taught and how the material is taught.

Although most schools have introduced teaching techniques that go beyond traditional drill and practice, the predominant instructional model continues to be a prescribed and presented approach to learning. The textbook, curriculum guide, or lists of standards dictate what is to be taught, and the material is presented to students in a predetermined, linear, and sequential manner. Educators have become more clever and imaginative in escaping the restrictiveness of highly structured deductive models, and it is not uncommon to see teachers using approaches such as discovery learning, simulations, cooperative learning, inquiry training, problem-based learning, and concept learning. More recent approaches include simulated problem solving through interactive computer technology. Some of these approaches certainly make learning more active and enjoyable than traditional, content-based deductive learning, but the bottom line is that there are certain predetermined bodies of information and thinking processes that students are expected to acquire. The instructional effects of the deductive model are those directly achieved by leading the learner in specific directions. As indicated above, there is nothing inherently "wrong" with the deductive model; however, it is based on a limited conception of the role of the learner. It fails to consider variations in interests, strengths, and learning preferences, and it always places students in the roles of lesson learners and exercise doers rather than authentic, firsthand inquirers.

THE INDUCTIVE MODEL OF LEARNING

The inductive model, on the other hand, represents the kinds of learning that ordinarily occurs outside formal classrooms in places such as research laboratories, artists' studios and theaters, film and video production sets, business offices, service agencies, and almost any extracurricular activity in which products, performances, or services are pursued. The names most closely associated with inductive learning are John Dewey, Maria Montessori, and Jerome Bruner. The type of learning advocated by these theorists can be defined as knowledge and skill acquisition gained from investigative and creative activities that are characterized by three requirements. First, there is a personalization of the topic or problem—the students are doing the work because they want to. Second, students are using methods of investigation or creative production that approximate the modus operandi of the practicing professional, even if the methodology is at a more junior level than that used by adult researchers, filmmakers, or business entrepreneurs. Third, the work is always geared toward the production of a product or service that is intended to have an impact on a particular audience. The information (content) and the skills (process) at the heart of inductive learning situations are based on need-to-know and need-to-do requirements.

For example, if a group of students is interested in examining differences in attitudes toward dress codes or teenage dating between and within various groups (e.g., gender, grade, students versus adults), they need certain background information. What have other studies on these topics revealed? Are there any national trends? Have other countries examined dress code or teenage dating issues? Where can these studies be found? Students will need to learn how to design authentic questionnaires, rating scales, and interview schedules and how to record, analyze, and report their findings in the most appropriate format (e.g., written, statistical, graphic, oral, dramatized). Finally, they will need to know how to identify potentially interested audiences, the most appropriate presentation formats (based on a particular audience's level of comprehension), and how to open doors for publication and presentation opportunities. This example demonstrates how knowledge and skills that might otherwise be considered trivial or unimportant become instantaneously relevant because they are necessary to prepare a high-quality product. All resources, information, schedules, and sequences of events are directed toward this goal, and evaluation is a function of the quality of the product or service as viewed through the eyes of a client, consumer, or other type of audience member. Everything that results in learning in a research laboratory, for example, is for present use. Therefore, looking up new information, conducting an experiment, analyzing results, or preparing a report is focused primarily on the present rather than the future. Even the amount of time devoted to a particular project cannot be determined in advance because the nature of the problem and the unknown obstacles that might be encountered prevent rigid schedules.

LEARNING THEORY 101 SUMMARIZED

The deductive model has dominated most formal education, and its track record has been less than impressive. One need only reflect for a moment on his or her own school experience to realize that with the exception of basic language and arithmetic, much of the compartmentalized material learned for some remote and ambiguous future situation is seldom used for daily activities. The names of famous generals, geometric formulas, the periodic table, and parts of a plant—learned outside an applicable, real-world situation—are usually quickly forgotten. This is not to say that previously learned information is unimportant, but its relevancy, meaningfulness, and retention is minimized when it is learned apart from situations that have personal value for the learner.

Inductive learning, on the other hand, focuses on the present use of content and processes as a way of integrating material and thinking skills into the more enduring structure of the learner's repertoire. It is these more enduring structures that have the greatest amount of transfer value for future use. When content and processes are learned in authentic, contextual situations, they result in more meaningful uses of information and problem-solving strategies than the learning that takes place in preparation-for-the-test situations. If individuals involved in inductive learning experiences receive some choice in the domains and activities in which they are engaged, and if the experiences are directed toward realistic and personalized goals, this type of learning has relevancy and meaning.

If people do, in fact, learn important content and skills outside of formal classroom situations, then it is important to examine the dimensions of real-world learning and the ways in which it can be brought into the school. However, bringing anything new into the school can be a tricky business. The track record in this regard has been one of overstructuring and institutionalizing even the most innovative approaches to learning. Many educators can remember how the much-heralded concept of discovery learning ended up being what one teacher called "sneaky telling" and how a focus on thinking skills and creative thinking fell prey to the same types of formulas and prescribed activities that characterized the content-based curriculum that has been criticized so strongly by thinking skills advocates. Even the present fascination with online learning is in some cases turning out to be little more than tutoring with electronic worksheets. But if we, as educators, can learn to view the Internet and other media as vast treasure chests of categorical and searchable information that can be sought out on a need-to-know basis, then we will begin to tap into the true value of this resource for inductive learning experiences.

HIGH-END LEARNING DEFINED

High-end learning is based on the ideas of a small number of philosophers, theorists, and researchers (e.g., John Dewey, Albert Bandura, Howard Gardner, Maria Montessori, Philip Phenix, Robert Sternberg, E. Paul Torrance, Alfred North Whitehead; for more information see Renzulli's *Schools for Talent Development*, 1994). The work of these theorists, coupled with our own research and program development activities, has given rise to the concept that we call *high-end learning*. The best way to define this concept is in terms of the following four guiding principles:

1. Each learner is unique, and, therefore, all learning experiences must be examined in ways that take into account the abilities, interests, and learning preferences of the individual.
2. Learning is more effective when students enjoy what they are doing. Consequently, learning experiences should be constructed and assessed with as much concern for enjoyment as for other goals.
3. Learning is more meaningful and enjoyable when content (i.e., facts) and process (e.g., thinking skills, methods of inquiry) are learned in the context of a real and present problem. Therefore, attention should be given to opportunities to personalize student choice in problem selection, the relevance of the problem for individuals and groups who share a common interest in the problem, and strategies for assisting students in personalizing problems they might choose to study.
4. Some formal instruction may be used in high-end learning, but a major goal of this approach is to enhance knowledge and thinking skill acquisition gained through teacher instruction with applications of knowledge and skills that result from student construction of meaningfulness.

Many educators have asked us to be more precise about the goals of enrichment clusters. They want answers to questions such as "What are the specific skills that define high-end learning?" and "How are these skills different from the traditional goals of deductive learning?" To address these questions, we used an inductive rather than deductive approach—that is, rather than making a list from the theoretical literature or our own expectations about goals and outcomes, we examined activities taking place in clusters, evaluated student work and teacher involvement, and drew conclusions based on these actual experiences. In other words, we did exactly what we are recommending students do as they go about pursuing problems in their enrichment clusters.

After carefully examining the work of numerous students and questioning many teachers who participated in the enrichment cluster research project, we were able to identify the following list of specific outcomes. Not all outcomes occurred in every cluster, and the levels to which any individual or group achieved these outcomes varied. Taken collectively, however, we believe that these learning behaviors represent a fairly comprehensive list of outcome goals. We recommend that you include such a list in your proposal for or description of an enrichment cluster program. The specific skills that are the goals of high-end learning include developing the ability to:

- find and focus a problem that has personal relevance to the individual or group;
- distinguish between problem-specific, relevant, and irrelevant information, identify bias in information sources, and transform factual information into usable knowledge that will help solve the problem;
- plan tasks that address the problem, sequence events in their most logical and practical order for attacking the problem, and consider alternative courses of action and their possible consequences;
- monitor one's understanding at each level of involvement and assess the need for gathering more advanced-level information (content), methodological skills (process), and human or material resources;
- notice patterns, relationships, and discrepancies in the information gathered and use this information to refine tasks for addressing the problem and drawing comparisons and analogies to other problems;
- generate reasonable arguments and explanations for each decision and course of action;
- predict outcomes; apportion time, money, and resources; value the contributions of others to the collective effort; and work cooperatively for the common good of the group;
- examine ways in which problem-solving strategies from one situation can be adopted in or adapted to other problem-solving situations (transfer of learning); and
- communicate in lively and professional ways to different audiences and in different genres and formats.

The ultimate goal of learning that is guided by the four principles and the specific goals or outcomes listed above is to replace dependence and passive learning with independence and engaged learning. Although all but the most conservative

[handwritten margin note: Goals of High-End Learning]

educators will agree with these principles and outcomes, much controversy exists about how these (or similar) principles and outcomes may be applied in everyday school situations. Some might view these principles as yet another abstract and generalized list of ideals that cannot be achieved in schools already overwhelmed by prescribed curriculum and deductive models of teaching. For this reason, we have provided guidelines for developing schedules that insert enrichment clusters into the regular school week without forcing out other activities (see Chapter 3: Seven Steps to Implementing an Enrichment Cluster Program). By setting aside a time and following a simple set of guidelines, educators can give all students opportunities to participate in high-end learning experiences sometime during their school week.

The most difficult part of facilitating high-end learning is guiding teachers to stop prescribing learning activities and curricular content and to replace traditional instruction with the kinds of "guide-on-the-side" responsibilities that are used by mentors and coaches. People in these roles instruct only when there is a direct need to accomplish a task necessary for developing a product or service. Many teachers who have served in extracurricular activities as yearbook advisors, drama club directors, 4-H Club advisors, or athletic coaches already have the techniques necessary for high-end learning. The following principles characterize extracurricular activities:

- Students and teachers select the area in which they participate.
- They produce products and/or services that are intended to have an impact on a particular audience.
- They use the authentic methods and advanced-level content of professionals to produce their product or service. They may operate at a more junior level than adult professionals, but their goal is exactly the same—to produce a product or service of as high quality as possible given their level of experience and the availability of resources.

The teacher's role in these activities is to guide students as they find and focus a real-world problem, lend a hand as they locate resources, and help them understand how to use their resources. For example, in a cluster that examined the incidence of acid rain in the northeastern part of the United States, the teacher taught students how to prepare slides for microscope analysis and, with the aid of a microprojector, showed them how to identify contaminants in their rainwater samples. Direct instruction should take place only when the acquisition of a new skill needs some explanation and demonstration by the teacher.

"REAL-WORLD PROBLEM" DEFINED

The term *real-world problem* has been tossed around so freely and easily in education circles these days that it has become little more than a hollow cliché. But a good deal of the focus of enrichment clusters is on the pursuit of real-world problems, and a precise definition of this oft-used but frequently elusive term is possible.

Enrichment clusters are designed to promote high-end learning, and a key concept in organizing and delivering services for this type of learning is application. *High-end learning consists of applying relevant knowledge, research skills, creative and critical thinking skills, and interpersonal skills to the solution of real problems.* But what makes a problem real? We define a real-world problem in terms of four essential elements:

1. Personalization of the problem. First, a real problem requires a personal frame of reference for the individual or group pursuing the problem. In other words, the problem must involve an emotional commitment to action in addition to a cognitive or scholarly interest or simple curiosity. Something that is a real problem for one individual or group may not be a real problem for others. For example, stating that global warming or urban crime are "real problems" does not make them real for an individual or group unless they decide to do something to address the problem. For these reasons, problems pursued in enrichment clusters must not be predetermined by the teacher or externally assigned. (An exception to this requirement might be an enrichment cluster formed around an established program, e.g., Math League.) Teachers may help in problem finding and focusing, but students within the cluster should be the main decision makers in selecting the problem and the ways in which it will be pursued. This self-selection provides the ownership and commitment that is needed to work on the development of a product or service for an extended period of time. Facilitators must avoid crossing the line from suggestion to prescription. Divisions of labor within clusters (discussed in Chapter 2: What Is an Enrichment Cluster?) allow individuals to specialize in some aspect of the problem and product, thus increasing opportunities for students to place a personal stamp on any given problem and product.

2. Open-endedness of the problem. A second essential element of real problems is that they do not have existing or unique solutions for the groups or individuals addressing the problem. If an agreed-upon solution or right answer already exists, then the cluster is more appropriately classified as a training exercise. Even simulations based on approximations of real-world events are considered training exercises if their main purpose is to teach predetermined content or thinking skills. Professionals solve problems in order to bring about some form of change in the actions, attitudes, or beliefs of a targeted audience, or because they want to contribute something new to the sciences, arts, humanities, or other areas of human productivity. We use the word "new" here in a local rather than global way. It is not necessary for young people to make contributions that are new for all humankind. Replications of studies that have been done many times before can be new in a relative sense if they are based on new data gathered locally or a new wrinkle in the data that makes the study different from the work of others. For example, a group of young people who gathered, analyzed, and reported on data about television watching habits in their community were contributing information that was new, in a local sense, even though similar studies had been done in other communities.

3. Authentic methods and advanced content. The third essential element of a real problem is that it be addressed using authentic methods that apply advanced content—that is, by employing the methodology, knowledge, and materials typically used by investigators and creative producers in the various disciplines. Enrichment clusters ask students to assume the roles of practicing professionals as they apply cutting-edge knowledge and content from the area of study. These roles and skills may be at a more junior level than adult journalists, historians, artists, environmentalists, filmmakers, or other professionals, but they are clearly different from the typical school role of student as lesson-learner. Using authentic methods is critical because one of the goals of inductive learning is to help young people extend their skills beyond the usual kinds of products that often result when teachers and students view "research" as merely looking up and reporting information. Authentic methodology lends itself to authentic products.

Similarly, in an enrichment cluster, students construct meaning and consult advanced references and sources as professionals would. Although some reporting of previously known information is a necessary part of most investigations—in the professional world, the pursuit of new knowledge should always begin with a review of what is already known about a given topic—the end result should be a creative contribution that goes beyond existing information that can be found in books or on the Internet. Every field of organized knowledge can be defined, in part, by its methodology, and the methodology of most fields can be found in certain kinds of guidebooks or manuals. These "how-to" books are the key to escalating studies beyond the traditional report writing approach that often passes for research. In later chapters, we describe examples of these books and the ways in which teachers can access various sources of methodological information. Likewise, the content of a field is often organized in books about the specific topic, found online and in current journals of the field. To obtain advanced knowledge, students and cluster facilitators alike can connect with experts in their areas of pursuit.

Every field of knowledge can also be defined in part by the kinds of data that represent the raw material of the field. New contributions are made in a field when investigators apply well-defined methods to the process of making sense out of random pieces of information. Although some investigations require levels of sophistication and equipment that are far beyond the reach of student investigators, almost every field of knowledge has entry-level and junior-level data-gathering opportunities.

4. Authentic audiences. The final essential element of real problems is that their solutions are directed toward real audiences. Real audiences are a major part of the *raison d'être* of the practicing professional upon which this model of learning and teaching is based. Professionals develop creative products for specific clients, and students within enrichment clusters also need to develop their work for a real audience. Audiences may change as the work evolves, but they serve as targets that give purpose and direction to the work. Any teacher who has been involved in the production of a school concert or play knows how anticipation of opening night focuses the preparation, precision, and quality of the performance. The same striving for excellence can be found in groups responsible for publishing a school newspaper or yearbook or developing a community action project. A sense of audience contributes greatly to task commitment and concern for excellence.

Real audiences consist of people who voluntarily attend to information, events, services, or objects. What one group of students did with the results of their local oral history project illustrates the difference between a real and a contrived audience. Although this group first presented its findings to classmates, it did so mainly to rehearse presentation skills. The group's authentic audience consisted of members of a local historical society and individuals who read about the student research in the local newspaper and a historical society newsletter.

THE ASSEMBLY PLANT OF THE MIND

Student-driven learning should achieve the following five objectives:

1. Students receive opportunities, resources, and encouragement to apply their interests, knowledge, thinking skills, creative ideas, and task commitment to self-selected problems or areas of study.
2. Students acquire advanced understanding of the knowledge and methodology used within particular disciplines, artistic areas of expression, and interdisciplinary studies.
3. Students develop authentic products or services that are directed primarily toward bringing about a desired impact on one or more specified audiences.
4. Students develop self-directed learning skills in the areas of planning, problem finding and focusing, organizational skills, resource utilization, time management, cooperativeness, decision making, and self-evaluation.

5.   Students develop task commitment, self-confidence, feelings of creative accomplishment, and the ability to interact effectively with other students and adults who share common goals and interests.

Student-driven learning focuses on the pursuit of real problems and should be viewed as the vehicle through which everything—from basic skills to advanced content and processes—comes together in the form of student-developed products and services. In much the same way that all the separate but interrelated parts of an automobile come together at an assembly plant, this form of learning constitutes an assembly plant of the mind. This kind of learning represents a synthesis and an application of content, process, and personal involvement. The student's role is transformed from one of lesson-learner to firsthand inquirer, and the role of the teacher changes from an instructor and disseminator of knowledge to a combination of coach, resource procurer, mentor, and, sometimes, a partner or colleague. Although products play an important role in creating these authentic learning situations, the development and application of a wide range of cognitive, affective, and motivational processes are the major goals of this type of learning.

KEY RESOURCES

This brief excursion through the complexities of learning theory and the thinking behind student-driven learning is important because it will help you understand the big picture of what we are trying to achieve through enrichment clusters. Although any change from the status quo is always a little intimidating at the start, we have achieved a fair amount of success by gaining faculty, administrative, and parental consensus on a small number of easy-to-understand concepts and related services and by providing resources and professional development related to specific service delivery procedures.

Enrichment clusters represent part of a general plan—called the Schoolwide Enrichment Model (SEM; Renzulli & Reis, 2014)—to develop the gifts and talents of all young people. Although enrichment clusters can be developed and implemented independently from the overall Schoolwide Enrichment Model, some of SEM's underlying theory, research, and practical know-how on developing gifts and talents can be useful to program developers, both as background information and for expanding the continuum of services based on this common goal. The following key resources provide valuable information about SEM and schoolwide enrichment in general:

Reis, S. M., Burns, D. E., & Renzulli, J. S. (1992). *Curriculum compacting: The complete guide to modifying the regular curriculum for high-ability students.* Waco, TX: Prufrock Press. This book shows teachers how to streamline the regular curriculum in order to provide time for more challenging enrichment and acceleration activities.

Renzulli, J. S. (1997). *Interest-A-Lyzer family of instruments: A manual for teachers.* Waco, TX: Prufrock Press. This manual describes six interest assessment instruments that invite students to examine present and potential interests, and explains how to administer and interpret these tools.

Kettle, K. E., Renzulli, J. S., & Rizza, M. G. (1998). Products of mind: Exploring student preferences for product development using My Way: An Expression Style Inventory. *Gifted Child Quarterly, 42*(1), pp. 48–61. "My Way" helps teachers and students determine which kind of products students are interested in creating.

Renzulli, J. S., & Reis, S. M. (2014). *The schoolwide enrichment model: A how-to guide for educational excellence (3rd ed.).* Waco, TX: Prufrock Press. This resource offers practical advice for achieving educational excellence in today's schools through a Schoolwide Enrichment Model program.

Finally, visit http://www.gifted.uconn.edu and click on the Schoolwide Enrichment Model link for more information and resources.

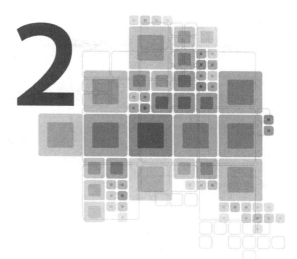

2

WHAT IS AN ENRICHMENT CLUSTER?

The whole process of education should thus be conceived of as the process of learning to think through the solutions of real problems.

—John Dewey

How can educators squeeze in time for the highly engaging learning activities that make schools enjoyable, creative, and challenging places for students (and staff) in the face of twin realities: the pressures to raise standardized test scores and the ever-growing lists of prescribed standards, required content, and performance outcomes? Research carried out with numerous schools across the country indicates that this seemingly impossible task can be achieved by inserting a block of time into the school week during which inductive learning is the major focus of student activity. In an enrichment cluster program, educators use this block of time to turn students' attention toward authentic learning applied to real-world problems.

ENRICHMENT CLUSTERS DEFINED AND EXEMPLIFIED

Enrichment clusters allow groups of students who share a common interest to come together each week during specially designated time blocks to produce a product, performance, or targeted service based on that common interest. Enrichment clusters usually last for 8–12 weeks. A series of clusters occurs in the beginning of the year, followed by a 4- or 5-week break and then another series in the second half of the school year. By having all clusters take place during a designated "cluster time," all teachers, specialists, and students can participate. Depending on the number of students who sign up for individual clusters, some offerings may be repeated, and if student and teacher interest warrants, other clusters may continue. Clusters that are repeated should not be carbon copies of the original cluster. The topic may remain the same and some of the start-up activities can be similar, but student choices for product development and the ways in which they go about their work should evolve according to each particular group's interests and needs. Like the work of a painter or composer, each cluster should create itself. The canvas or the score sheet may remain the same, but each painting or composition is a new creation. Each cluster should be seen as an original. Otherwise, there is a danger of slipping back into a deductive mode of teaching.

Teachers or other adults who have a special interest in a particular topic facilitate the clusters. Students with advanced knowledge and interest in a specialized area can also serve as cluster facilitators, working in cooperation with teachers or other adults if necessary. (Student-led clusters have been most effective when older students work with younger groups, and we suggest a separation of at least three grade levels between student facilitators and students in the cluster.) All facilitators, including students and community volunteers, should receive orientation and training to help them develop a clear understanding of the difference between deductive and inductive learning. Many of the staff development activities in Chapter 5: Staff Development and Program Evaluation can be used to orient community volunteers as well as to prepare educators.

As mentioned earlier, clusters are modeled after the ways in which knowledge acquisition and application take place in real-world situations. In clusters, students make use of relevant knowledge and apply thinking skills to common problems identified by the group. The Video Production Company illustrates how students learn in their quest to address an identified problem with an authentic product or service.

THE VIDEO PRODUCTION COMPANY

Bill Bonfante, a middle school history teacher, had nurtured a strong interest in filmmaking and video production since his college days, when he was involved in a number of theater and video production activities. When the enrichment cluster program started, he wrote a description for a group he wanted to facilitate:

The Video Production Company

Are you a video buff? Do you love history? Ever wonder how film-makers create their films? If so, this cluster is for you! Come and chart a course for an exciting video production adventure. The only requirement is your love of film and history. Bring the past to life through the magic of filmmaking!

Sixteen students from sixth through eighth grade selected this cluster because they were drawn to areas listed in the description. Early meetings of the group focused on selecting a topic for their first production, deciding who would work in the various subgroups (writing, filming, editing, etc.) and what their responsibilities would be, and setting up a sequence of events. After a few brainstorming sessions, the group decided to make a documentary about the Battles of Lexington and Concord and Paul Revere's ride. The target audiences for the video would be fourth graders who study this topic in their history class and other Revolutionary War buffs who would watch their video on YouTube.

Mr. Bonfante showed short segments of films and videos dealing with histori-cal topics and invited a parent who was a local television producer to talk with the group. He located several how-to sites dealing with script writing, storyboarding, filming techniques, costumes, make-up, and of course, historical descriptions of the battles and Paul Revere's famous ride. Students spent most of cluster time (90-minute sessions once a week) in small task groups, with short whole-group meetings to report progress and make entries on the master production schedule. In addition to a director who coordinated the overall shooting, two students served as producers, with responsibility for recruiting extras, locating and gaining permis-sion for shooting, arranging transportation, recruiting parents for costume making, and acquiring resources (including a horse and rider).

As the facilitator of the cluster, Mr. Bonfante helped students focus the prob-lem from a general area of interest (video production) to a specific topic (the bat-tles and Paul Revere's ride). He also helped identify the jobs to be done, obtain the required resources, and develop an action plan. He worked with the group on developing interpersonal skills, running effective meetings, and managing time. These activities were always student driven, with Mr. Bonfante playing an advisory role.

Wherever possible, Mr. Bonfante encouraged students to imitate or model the roles and responsibilities carried out by actual professionals working in the field of video production. References to how-to books or phone calls to individuals in the profession sought answers to questions such as "How can you make a shoot during the day look like night?", "Where can we find out which British regiments fought here and what their uniforms looked like?", and "How can you make a church in one location look like it is next to a body of water that is in another location?"

Division of labor enabled all students to have ownership of a component of the production and to find a niche that complemented their individual strengths, interests, and expression styles.

Although various levels of talent and leadership emerged in the task groups, Mr. Bonfante continually emphasized that each person's specialty area was valuable because of its essential contribution to the whole project. At all times his role was to support and escalate the level of each subgroup's work without taking over or assertively directing the tasks. Like a coach, he used his experience to offer advice in the form of possible alternatives, predict problems and needs, arbitrate differences of opinion, and maximize students' opportunities for decision making. This role required a great deal of patience and restraint. He allowed students to struggle and experience frustration in order to turn challenges and setbacks into successes. He recognized that students must "own the problem" if they are ultimately to achieve the goals set forth in Chapter 1: Freedom to Teach and feel genuine satisfaction in their success. As the work of the Video Production Company evolved, Mr. Bonfante turned more and more responsibilities over to the students, and in many cases, he became adept at answering a question with a question.

Behind the real action of the cluster, Mr. Bonfante worked what might be called the politics of enrichment clusters. He spent some time examining the state's content standards so that he could document the value of his cluster as related to those standards. He connected appropriate standards to various cluster activities and developed informal criteria to document and determine student growth in various content standard areas. As Table 2.1 shows, his cluster clearly addressed both Common Core and the state's standards in a naturally appealing format for students and the facilitator. Notice the subtle differences in the Common Core standards listed across grade levels for ELA-Litearcy.RL.6.7, ELA-Literacy.RL.7.7, and ELA-Literacy.RI.8.7. This structure lends itself well to multiage groupings of students.

GUIDELINES FOR ENRICHMENT CLUSTERS

There are eight guidelines that differentiate an enrichment cluster from a traditional course, minicourse, or unit of instruction. These guidelines can serve as a checklist to evaluate whether or not a cluster is based on an inductive model of teaching and learning.

1. Focus on application of content and process. This first guideline—the Golden Rule of enrichment clusters—demands that all cluster activity be directed toward making a product, performance, or service for an authentic audience. All learning that takes place within the cluster is pursued for application purposes,

TABLE 2.1

COMMON CORE AND STATE STANDARDS ADDRESSED BY VIDEO PRODUCTION COMPANY

	6th Grade	7th Grade	8th Grade
COMMON CORE STANDARDS			
Reading	1.) CCSS.ELA-Literacy.RL.6.7 Compare and contrast the experience of reading a story, drama, or poem to listening to or viewing an audio, video, or live version of the text, including contrasting what they "see" and "hear" when reading the text to what they perceive when they listen or watch.	1.) CCSS.ELA-Literacy.RL.7.7 Compare and contrast a written story, drama, or poem to its audio, filmed, staged, or multimedia version, analyzing the effects of techniques unique to each medium (e.g., lighting, sound, color, or camera focus and angles in a film).	1.) CCSS.ELA-Literacy.RI.8.7 Evaluate the advantages and disadvantages of using different media (e.g., print or digital text, video, multimedia) to present a particular topic or idea.
Reading	2.) CCSS.ELA-Literacy.RI.6.10 By the end of the year, read and comprehend literary nonfiction in the grades 6–8 text complexity band proficiently, with scaffolding as needed at the high end of the range.	2.) CCSS.ELA-Literacy.RI.7.10 By the end of the year, read and comprehend literary nonfiction in the grades 6–8 text complexity band proficiently, with scaffolding as needed at the high end of the range.	2.) CCSS.ELA-Literacy.RI.8.10 By the end of the year, read and comprehend literary nonfiction at the high end of the grades 6–8 text complexity band independently and proficiently.
Reading	3.) CCSS.ELA-Literacy.RI.6.7 Integrate information presented in different media or formats (e.g., visually, quantitatively) as well as in words to develop a coherent understanding of a topic or issue.	3.) CCSS.ELA-Literacy.RL.7.7 Compare and contrast a written story, drama, or poem to its audio, filmed, staged, or multimedia version, analyzing the effects of techniques unique to each medium (e.g., lighting, sound, color, or camera focus and angles in a film).	3.) CCSS.ELA-Literacy.RL.8.10 By the end of the year, read and comprehend literature, including stories, dramas, and poems, at the high end of grades 6–8 text complexity band independently and proficiently.
Speaking and Listening	1.) CCSS.ELA-Literacy.SL.6.1 Engage effectively in a range of collaborative discussions (one-on-one, in groups, and teacher-led) with diverse partners on grade 6 topics, texts, and issues, building on others' ideas and expressing their own clearly.	1.) CCSS.ELA-Literacy.SL.7.2 Analyze the main ideas and supporting details presented in diverse media and formats (e.g., visually, quantitatively, orally) and explain how the ideas clarify a topic, text, or issue under study.	1.) CCSS.ELA-Literacy.SL.8.3 Delineate a speaker's argument and specific claims, evaluating the soundness of the reasoning and relevance and sufficiency of the evidence and identifying when irrelevant evidence is introduced.
Speaking and Listening	2.) CCSS.ELA-Literacy.SL.6.5 Include multimedia components (e.g., graphics, images, music, sound) and visual displays in presentations to clarify information.	2.) CCSS.ELA-Literacy.SL.7.5 Include multimedia components and visual displays in presentations to clarify claims and findings and emphasize salient points.	2.) CCSS.ELA-Literacy.SL.8.5 Integrate multimedia and visual displays into presentations to clarify information, strengthen claims and evidence, and add interest.

TABLE 2.1, CONTINUED

Writing	CCSS.ELA-Literacy.W.6.7 Conduct short research projects to answer a question, drawing on several sources and refocusing the inquiry when appropriate.	CCSS.ELA-Literacy.W.7.3 Write narratives to develop real or imagined experiences or events using effective technique, relevant descriptive details, and well-structured event sequences.	CCSS.ELA-Literacy.W.8.8 Gather relevant information from multiple print and digital sources, using search terms effectively; assess the credibility and accuracy of each source; and quote or paraphrase the data and conclusions of others while avoiding plagiarism and following a standard format for citation.
STATE STANDARDS			
Social Studies	*Geography and culture.* A student shall demonstrate understanding of how regions of the world are defined in terms of location, resources, people and culture, and physical features; and how global systems are interconnected		
	History and citizenship. A student shall demonstrate knowledge of the facts and sequences of historical events, the origins and shaping influences of various points of view, and historical events in relationship to themes of change and migration		
Science	*Direct observation.* A student shall demonstrate the ability to gather information to answer a scientific or social science question		
	Accessing information. A student shall access information and use a variety of sources to answer a question or support a position		
The Arts	*Artistic creativity and performance.* A student shall demonstrate knowledge of art forms through artistic process and presentation		
Technology	*Technology applications.* A student shall use appropriate technology to access, evaluate, and organize information and to produce products		

whether that learning involves content acquisition, the use of thinking processes, or the development of leadership skills, inter- or intrapersonal skills, organizational and time management skills, or any other desirable educational outcome. This type of learning is what John Dewey (1939) called "collateral learning," and its value is derived from the fact that whatever is learned is instantly relevant because it is necessary to address a particular problem. The most enduring and transferable outcomes of this type of learning are the processes themselves, but products, performances, and services are the essential and defining elements of an enrichment cluster. Because they are important outcomes of enrichment clusters, we have included an overview of cognitive and affective processes (Renzulli & Reis, 1997) in Figure 2.1. This information can help you think about a range of data process goals for clusters. However, just as you want to avoid overspecifying content objectives, you will also want to avoid overspecifying process outcomes. If overspecification is not avoided, a cluster might end up focusing on activities like "Today's Worksheet on Detecting Bias in Text." Inductive teaching requires that process skills evolve as a result of product or service development requirements. The taxonomy is included

---

Taxonomy of Cognitive and Affective Processes

I.   Cognitive and Affective Thinking
     A. Creative Thinking Skills
     B. Creative Problem Solving and Decision Making
     C. Critical and Logical Thinking

II. Character Development and Affective Process Skills
     A. Character Development
     B. Interpersonal Skills
     C. Intrapersonal Skills

III. Learning How To Learn Skills
     A. Listening, Observing, and Perceiving
     B. Reading, Notetaking, and Outlining
     C. Interviewing and Surveying
     D. Analyzing and Organizing

IV. Using Advanced Research Skills and Reference Materials
     A. Preparing for Research and Investigative Projects
     B. Library and Electronic Reference
     C. Finding and Using Community Resources

V.   Written, Oral, and Visual Communication Skills
     A. Written Communication Skills
     B. Oral Communication Skills
     C. Visual Communication Skills

FIGURE 2.1. Taxonomy of cognitive and affective processes. From *The Schoolwide Enrichment Model* (pp. 161–167) by J. S. Renzulli and S. M. Reis, 1997, Waco, TX: Prufrock Press. Copyright 1997 by Prufrock Press. Adapted with permission.

---

for general orientation purposes, to help teachers explain the purposes of clusters to students and parents and as a checklist to evaluate the cluster at its conclusion.

We have also included Handout 3.1c: Product Planning Guide (see Chapter 5: Staff Development and Program Evaluation) to help teachers explore a wide range of possible products in the following five areas of product development: Artistic Products, Performance Products, Spoken Products, Written Products, and Models/Construction Products. These lists have proven helpful to both teachers and students as they went about exploring the many options for expressing their work in creative ways.

2. Allow students and teachers to select the clusters in which they wish to participate. Research and common sense indicate that people learn better when they enjoy what they are doing, and a large part of enjoyment comes from being able to make selections from a number of available alternatives. When it comes to formal schooling, however, students have few opportunities to make choices. They may not know where their interests lie, giving them difficulty in making selections. Several self-assessment instruments from the family of Interest-A-Lyzers (Renzulli, 1997) help students get in touch with potential interests through a series of open-ended questions.

Because of the emphasis that enrichment clusters place on product or service development, it is also worthwhile to help students examine their preferences for various modes of expression. Some students are already aware of their preferences, especially if they have been involved in musical or artistic productions or in extracurricular activities that require a particular form of expression (e.g., school newspaper, art club). Other students will make more meaningful cluster choices if they are able to examine expression options, and even students with already established preferences might discover new avenues of expression through a self-analysis experience. To help students explore, we recommend using My Way ... An Expression Style Instrument (Kettle, Renzulli, & Rizza, 1998). This instrument, like the Interest-A-Lyzers, is not a test, and there are no norms or right or wrong answers. Rather, My Way helps young people understand their preferences and make better choices when given opportunities to participate in self-selected learning experiences.

It is not necessary to use these instruments with all students, but this process has helped students who are having difficulty choosing a cluster in which to participate. We have also found that after two or three series of clusters, readministering these instruments can help students stretch into new areas of interest and expression.

Outside of enrichment clusters, interest and expression style assessments can provide classroom teachers with valuable information about their students. This information can help teachers direct students into independent and small-group investigations in the general classroom. Additionally, information concerning students' interests and product/audience preferences can help teachers develop differentiated and tiered lessons. We suggest keeping information in a talent portfolio that can be easily accessed, such as the Total Talent Portfolio (Purcell & Renzulli, 1998), so that interest-based options can be explored when students complete classwork early or when there are opportunities in the regular classroom for self-selected activities. These instruments can also provide more general information. When viewed in groups, interest inventories provide information about what types of clusters ought to be offered, and expression inventories help facilitators understand the range of product/service/audience options that exists for cluster outcomes.

Effective teaching takes place when teachers bring their own personal excitement, enthusiasm, and commitment into the classroom. Therefore, the same philosophy that guides student interests also applies to teachers and other adults who might facilitate enrichment clusters. In our early experimentation with enrichment clusters, we found that many middle school teachers assumed that they should design clusters in the subject area in which they were currently teaching. These choices may be the best decisions for some teachers, but we also found that many teachers had interests and even strong passions for topics or areas of study outside their field that they always dreamed of applying to learning situations with young people who share similar interests. To help teachers explore potential areas for developing their own unique clusters, we used a self-assessment instrument entitled "Inspiration" (Gentry & Renzulli, 1995). This instrument explores special interests and activities that may serve as idea generators for cluster development. The instrument is printed here as Handout 3.1a: Inspiration Survey (see Chapter 5: Staff Development and Program Evaluation). It helps teachers identify colleagues with complementary interests, allowing them to explore opportunities for working together. For example, a teacher with a strong interest in local history and another interested in creative writing might choose to team up for a cluster on historical fiction and dramatizations about early settlers in their region.

A small amount of time invested in interest and expression style assessment will contribute greatly to the success of a cluster program. We know from our own experience as both teachers and students that the classes we enjoyed the most, the classes in which we were most engaged, and the classes in which we usually learned the most were the ones in which the teachers and students shared strong interests.

3. Group students across grade levels by interest areas. Most of students' school lives are spent with age and grade peers, but in the out-of-school world, people are almost always grouped by interest or common task areas. Because enrichment clusters make every effort to follow a real-world pattern of organization and learning, we strongly recommend that cluster enrollment range across two to three grade levels (and we have seen successful clusters that included four grade levels). In addition to providing a real-world environment, grouping students by interests allows for what scientists call a "critical mass"—bringing together as many of the necessary ingredients as possible to produce the best results. In a learning situation, more creative and dynamic interactions take place if a larger number of students with a common interest work together rather than separating the group just because they happen to be of different ages. Age becomes imperceptible when there are strong commonalities of interest, and many benefits result when, for example, a younger student's unpolished but creative idea is teamed up with an older student's know-how or extended experience in a certain segment of the task. There is also a very practical reason for cross-grade grouping. In one of the elementary schools involved in our research, a marvelous enrichment cluster in fashion design was offered across grades three through five. Because of time constraints and the availability of only one teacher who wanted to offer this cluster, it would have been impossible to have Fashion Design for Third Graders, Fashion Design for Fourth Graders, etc. In addition, the cluster would have lost the excitement and enthusiasm that 22 engaged students generated.

4. Do not use predetermined unit or lesson plans. This guideline is perhaps the most difficult for beginning cluster facilitators to deal with, and yet it is crucial to follow if teachers are to prevent regression to a deductive model of learning that turns enrichment clusters into minicourses. The absence of unit or lesson plans does not mean that there are no guidelines for general start-up activities, and we will discuss these guidelines in Chapter 4: How to Develop Your Own Enrichment Cluster.

During early experimentation with the enrichment cluster concept, we encountered a tendency for some facilitators to turn the clusters into minicourses. Minicourses are designed to teach prescribed content or thinking skills to students (the deductive model). Minicourses may differ from regular instructional units in that they deal with topics not ordinarily covered in the regular curriculum, and they may use teaching strategies that are different from traditional recitation, drill, and testing practices. However, the ultimate purpose of most minicourses is to put into the heads of students a preselected set of content and/or process objectives. Although this goal is not unworthy, enrichment clusters offer students and educators something different—something more student-centered.

It bears repeating that all activities taken on by an enrichment cluster should be necessary to solve a real problem that has been identified by the students. Students learn new material within the context of an authentic and present problem. In enrichment clusters, teachers must purposefully avoid prespecifying content or process objectives in order to allow students to follow the investigative methods of practicing professionals in the real world. If teachers approach clusters by prespecifying what and how students are going to learn, they would return to teaching practices that typify regular instruction.

Planning an enrichment cluster is, in many ways, an easier and more natural process than planning for traditional teaching. Cluster facilitators need only determine (through discussions with students) a problem, a product or service that addresses the problem, and an intended audience, and then take the steps necessary to acquire the resources and knowledge needed to produce the product or deliver the service. Information, materials, problem-solving skills, and assistance automatically become relevant because students require them to make the product or deliver the service. Imagine for a moment all of the things about arithmetic, geometry, geography, architecture, purchasing, aesthetics, computer graphics, advertising, photography, accounting, cooperation, leadership, and ornithology that a group of elementary grade students can learn simply by deciding that they want to design, construct, and market environmentally friendly birdhouses and feeders!

A good deal of teacher training demands that educators begin by first stating objectives and learning outcomes and then designing lessons to achieve those objectives, but enrichment clusters are modeled after natural (nonschool) learning. The traditional approach to pedagogy can be a difficult habit to break. We hope that the suggestions in Chapter 4: How to Develop Your Own Enrichment Cluster will serve as a guide for using an inductive approach to pedagogy rather than the prescribed and presented approach that characterizes most regular curriculum and minicourse activities.

Engaging students in advanced, interesting, and challenging content is an essential feature of enrichment clusters. However, a second problem we encountered in our research on enrichment clusters was a failure on the parts of some facilitators to escalate the level of knowledge pursued within a cluster. Hands on should not mean brains off! We observed many exciting, fun-filled activities, and this kind of enjoyment in learning is unquestionably one of the most desirable features of a good cluster. At the same time, some critics decried certain clusters as being nothing more than "fun and games," and others have said that the clusters are "soft on content" and that they don't represent "real school." Cluster facilitators can guard against these criticisms by examining each cluster with an eye toward what constitutes authentic and rigorous content within the field or fields of study around which the cluster is organized. For example, in the birdhouse cluster group mentioned earlier, the facilitator began by helping students identify credible Internet resources on ornithology, marketing, and advertising, as well as birdhouse and feeder construction. He also worked with the librarian to identify some print resources and books on these topics. The students studied maps to learn about birds indigenous to their area of the country and their migratory habits, learned about the birds' anatomy in order to determine how big to make the birdhouses and openings, and studied different preferred diets, colors, mating habits, and optimal locations. Students prepared a website and a Facebook page with attractive drawings and photographs to help market their products, and a subgroup within the cluster interested in desktop publishing produced printed material to accompany each birdhouse and feeder that was sold. The students became specialists in the various subtopics, the tasks required to develop high-quality products, and the procedures for researching, constructing, and marketing their products. This pursuit of advanced content helps avoid the "soft on content" criticism that is inevitable in an age when standards and test scores are of primary concern to education leaders, and it is one of the reasons why we encourage students and cluster facilitators to document all advanced resources used in their work. Although high-quality products are the best evidence of student achievement, even a list of advanced resources and reference materials used, websites accessed, and resource contacts who contributed know-how will assist in documenting the level of rigor in the cluster.

Another example of content escalation comes from a cluster on fashion design. Although the cluster focused mainly on designing clothing for teens, the students researched 100 years of fashion trends by decade and presented their findings on a history of fashion website. This historical analysis provided both a scholarly perspective to their work and generated creative ideas about the fashions they were currently developing. A real need for background information and the know-how for getting it (e.g., old magazines, Montgomery Ward and Sears Roebuck catalogs) raised the level of academic authenticity.

Making sure students pursue higher levels of knowledge and professional methodology is a key role for the cluster facilitator. Although the facilitator does not need to be an expert in content areas beforehand, it is necessary for him or her to:

- have an interest in the topic and a "feel" for content escalation;
- know how and where to find the resources that will advance the level of study;
- organize cluster activities so that knowledge escalation is pursued as part and parcel of the hands-on activities; and
- document the extent and level of advanced content that was pursued in the cluster.

Left to their own devices, the students in the birdhouse cluster might have skipped the underlying research in ornithology and marketing in favor of sawing, hammering, and painting. The fashion design group might have missed the opportunity to develop advanced research skills and a broader perspective on their area of interest. If this were the case, the cluster experiences would have lacked higher levels of learning and could easily have fallen prey to the "fun and games" criticism. In the birdhouse cluster, the facilitator's suggestion that "a good marketing strategy" would be to include a user's guide in each birdhouse and feeder created a genuine need to do the research in ornithology that raised the scholarly level of the enrichment cluster. The teacher did not instruct the students in ornithology, but rather, guided them toward finding the information they needed from sourcebooks and the Internet to create their final products. We call this kind of search for resources just-in-time information: It is instantly relevant because it is needed to address a real and present problem. In many ways, these examples underscore the most important role of the facilitator. The escalation process demands more than merely guiding the hands-on aspects of a cluster; it requires the facilitator to offer creative suggestions about the direction of cluster work that guarantee that academic growth is a hallmark of the cluster. Further discussion of this process can be found in Chapter 4: How to Develop Your Own Enrichment Cluster in a section on ensuring the scholarliness of enrichment clusters.

5. Help students access and apply authentic methods, advanced content, and the materials that professionals use. Most teachers can easily help students locate information about general and specific topics. In addition to the usual introductory resources, access to the Internet and the marvelous capabilities of search engines make a vast amount of information available to students of all ages. Unfortunately, far too many students believe that the only method for preparing a research project is to look up information using Wikipedia or Google. Looking up and making appropriate use of relevant background information is an important part of investigative work, but if it is the only method used, the end result is usually a report rather than authentic research. In order to engage in authentic research, teachers and students need to learn how to find and use methodological resources. We frequently refer to these resources as *how-to books*, *how-to sites*, or *Mentors-in-Print*, and they are essential for escalating studies beyond the traditional report-writing approach that often passes for research.

A how-to book or manual supplies information on how professionals in a particular field of study carry out investigative, creative, or action-oriented work. The following paragraph from *Understanding History: A Primer of Historical Method* (Gottschalk, 1969) pinpoints the unique function of these resources:

> The beginner, with or without aid, can easily discover a subject that interests him and that will be worthy of investigation—at least at an introductory level. He needs only to ask himself four sets of questions:
>
> The first set of questions is geographical. They center around the interrogative: "Where?" What area of the world do I wish to investigate? The Far East? Brazil? My country? My city? My neighborhood?
>
> The second set of questions is biographical. They center around the interrogative: "Who?" What persons am I interested in? The Chinese? The Greeks? My ancestors? My neighbors? A famous individual?
>
> The third set of questions is chronological. They center around the interrogative: "When?" What period of the past do I wish to study? From the beginnings till now? The fifth century B.C.? The Middle Ages? The 1780s? Last year?
>
> The fourth set of questions is functional or occupational. They center around the interrogative: "What?" What spheres of human interest concern me most? What kinds of human activity? Economics? Literature? Athletics? Gender? Politics? (pp. 62–63)

Figure 2.2 lists how-to books from a variety of disciplines. Note once again that the titles themselves often clearly reveal the aim of the book. These and other books are listed in Appendix C: Methodological Resources, but they are just a few of the hundreds of resources that focus on the how-to or investigative methodology of various subject matter areas. Most of them were written for young audiences or introductory investigators, and in most cases, they can be used as resource guides for students as well as adults who are facilitating a cluster. Cluster facilitators can

---

A Teen's Guide to Getting Published
A Teen's Guide to Creating Web Pages and Blogs
Animation Unleashed
Go: A Kidd's Guide to Graphic Design
Break a Leg: The Kids' Guide to Acting and Stagecraft
The Art of Construction
Engineering the City
Hands-On Archaeology
Filmmaking for Teens
Screenwriting for Teens
Creating History Documentaries
Public Speaking
The Kids' Book of Weather Forecasting
The Kids' Guide to Digital Photography
Making Handmade Books
Making Shadow Puppets
The Kids' Guide to Service Projects
Crime Scene Detective

FIGURE 2.2. Sample how-to titles.

---

also raise the level of rigor by obtaining introductory college-level texts and syllabuses in disciplines such as psychology, sociology, and biology. These syllabuses and books are especially helpful for identifying basic principles, major concepts, and the types of topics that are typically studied in a particular discipline. Some of these books also include laboratory manuals that guide students through actual research activities in particular fields of study, and syllabuses often contain links to the most recent innovations in the field. Cluster facilitators can also ask professionals in various fields for recommendations, although they should be sure to mention the ages of their students so that recommended resources are appropriate for younger investigators.

The Internet contains a wealth of methodological information and is an essential educational tool. A teacher facilitating a cluster on local history helped his students prepare for interviews with Vietnam veterans by using what he described as "three clicks on the Web." Starting with Google, he searched "oral history," which brought him to the Oral History Association website (http://www.oralhistory.org) and http://www.dohistory.org, which has its own tool kit. In addition, the search yielded the Smithsonian Folklife and Oral History Interviewing Guide (http://www.folklife.si.edu/education_exhibits/resources/guide/introduction.aspx). These outstanding resources were on the first page of the search results. What followed included university websites, data websites, and suggestions for how to engage in quality oral history. The world of advanced information is literally at our fingertips, and facilitators can use it to escalate the level of content and investigative methodology in enrichment clusters and in all teaching activities.

As we have mentioned before, almost every field of knowledge has entry-level and junior-level data-gathering opportunities. We have seen scientifically respectable questionnaire studies on food and television preferences carried out by primary-grade students. A group of middle-school students gathered and analyzed water samples as part of a large regional study on the extent and effects of acid rain. This work was so thoroughly and carefully done that the students' findings were requested by a state environmental agency. Another group of elementary students used very professional techniques in every aspect of producing a weekly television show broadcast by a local cable company. A fifth-grade student wrote a guidebook that was adopted by his city's government as the official historical walking tour of the city. He has developed an app that can be downloaded to a smartphone for an official tour. A group of high school students engaged in a very sophisticated community research and citizens' action project that resulted in the appropriation of $200,000 for a citywide system of bike paths. The success reflected in these examples can be traced to the proper use of authentic methods and techniques, even if these techniques were carried out at a somewhat junior level.

The facilitator's role in providing methodological assistance is to help students identify, locate, and obtain resource materials and/or persons that can help them with the appropriate use of investigative techniques. In some cases, cluster facilitators may need to consult with librarians or professionals within various fields for advice about where and how to find methodological resources. Facilitators may also need help from professionals in translating complex concepts into material students can understand. Although methodological assistance is a major part of the facilitator's responsibility, it is neither necessary nor realistic to expect facilitators to have mastered a large number of investigative techniques. A solid general background and orientation toward the overall nature of research is necessary, but the most important skills are the ability to know where and how to help students obtain the right material and the willingness to reach out beyond the usual school resources for specialized materials and resource persons.

6. Provide opportunities to develop multiple talents within an enrichment cluster through division of labor. In enrichment clusters, each student does not do the same tasks. There is a division of labor that models real-world productivity, and everyone contributes in his or her own area of interest and developing specialization. The group is connected by a common purpose, but each member makes a unique contribution to the overall enterprise. This guideline is easier to understand and implement by examining how various tasks are carried out in a business, theater production company, publishing enterprise, or community action agency. A dramatic or musical production group, for example, requires some people to fill the obvious functions (actors, producers, directors), but many others in more background roles are necessary to create a professional production. Scriptwriters, set designers and builders, business managers, costume designers, light and sound technicians, make-up specialists, and those who prepare advertising and publicity pieces all perform functions directed toward one goal—the final show. Because not all students perform the same tasks, enrichment clusters make it possible for a group of students with different achievement levels to work together. Students of varying abilities can work in the same cluster and all be challenged appropriately as long as they are allowed to contribute to the development of the product or service in a way that makes the most of their individual interests and strengths. Allowing students to pursue different tasks all aimed at a common goal also encourages interdependence, cooperation, and appreciation of others' strengths and talents.

The division of labor concept is valuable in cluster planning because it encourages teachers to help young people explore multidimensional projects. We have examined so-called enrichment clusters that amounted to little more than each student preparing a fairly traditional report on the migratory habits of his or her bird of choice. But imagine how teaming up field observers, photographers, writers, artists, and researchers could easily develop a broad range of talents and teamwork. Further imagine other talents in graphics, media, desktop publishing, teaching, and marketing that could be developed if the group decided to create a website, an app for local birdwatchers, and birdwatching workshops for other students or adults.

Although an enrichment cluster might have students working on different jobs contributing to the same end product or service, it is not uncommon to have several different outcomes within a single cluster. Individuals or small groups of students might choose to move in divergent directions within the general topic area, thus creating several different products and services within a single cluster. A theater group or a newspaper office might be focused on a single product, with different students carrying out different jobs that contribute to that one product, whereas an artists' guild might have individual artists each preparing a personal exhibit of their original works for a community arts festival. One enrichment cluster might generate a number of very different products and services. In one cluster on anime, some students developed their own anime cartoons using computer software; others chose to teach the art of drawing anime characters to primary students; and yet another group published a book that chronicled the origins and history of anime.

Once the cluster has started, a field trip to or a visiting speaker from a local business, laboratory, production company, or other organization can be a good source of information for determining the range of participation opportunities within any general area of interest. Asking questions about different jobs, responsibilities, and products or services will quickly help students identify particular roles that students might like to fulfill. A little background work will help facilitators include a range of the possible types of involvement in their cluster descriptions. A phone call, visit, or even a casual conversation with someone who works in the general area around which you want to develop a cluster will provide the kind of insider information that may not be apparent to people outside the field.

Facilitators must carefully craft cluster descriptions with consideration for all the possible roles and potential outcomes that might emerge once students arrive and begin to shape the cluster. Simply creating a description for a theater cluster that calls for actors would leave the cluster in short supply of set designers, directors, writers, and publicity people. Similar problems might emerge with a newschannel guild that only attracts reporters. Does the following description serve to attract a variety of potentially talented and interested students?

> Magazine Production Company
> Are you interested in photography, writing, computer graphics, cartooning, editing, layout, or marketing? If so, then becoming part of a cluster to develop an important and original magazine might be just the thing for you.

7. Set aside designated time blocks for enrichment clusters. Student-driven learning can take place in any classroom, but the pressures imposed by top-down curricular requirements and today's emphasis on preparation for standardized tests place limits on the amount of inductive learning that can take place in most classrooms. In order to guarantee that all students have opportunities for real-world, high-end learning, we recommend that schools set aside specially designated time blocks during the week when inductive learning is "on the front burner" of all students' learning experiences. We found that a block of time ranging from a double period to one half-day per week will provide the time necessary for effective clusters. Scheduling all of the clusters at the same time allows for total faculty availability and the opportunity to create the critical masses of interested students.

Before modifying the schedule, school leaders should bear two considerations in mind. First, teachers, administrators, students, and parents must value this type of learning. Administrator support and leadership is critical to successful, sustainable programs. If it is looked upon as a frill rather than something that contributes positive skills to the overall repertoire of the developing young person, a proposal for an enrichment cluster program will meet with a great deal of resistance. Creating appreciation for the type of learning advocated in enrichment clusters requires thoughtful sharing of information about the goals of inductive learning with the entire school family. Every person involved in an enrichment cluster program—especially teachers (who will be responsible for facilitating most of the clusters)—should be able to participate in discussions on the educational value of inductive learning. It is important in these discussions not to pit inductive learning against contemporary concerns about standards and the school's overall goal to improve achievement test scores. Both goals of schooling are important and should be viewed as complementary rather than competitive. Early discussions should focus on value issues so that groups do not get bogged down in practical implementation concerns, which can be considered once a decision has been made to go ahead with the program. Many good ideas for improving teaching and learning have been derailed because early negativity about "why we can't do it" has been placed in front of "why we should do it." Good capacity building requires that a majority of the participants agrees that an enrichment cluster program fits with its vision of a great school. If a majority of the faculty agrees about the value of an enrichment cluster program, implementation will be much easier, and creative solutions to practical concerns will emerge in later discussions on program development.

A second and more challenging practical consideration is scheduling itself. When is the best time to schedule enrichment clusters? Once a commitment has been made to the value of this type of learning, the entire faculty should carefully examine the overall weekly schedule in order to brainstorm creative suggestions. Ideas might range from a regularly scheduled time block each week to rotating time blocks and even afterschool programs. Each scheduling option has advantages and disadvantages, and scheduling options should be approached on a trial basis. If one approach to scheduling doesn't work, school leaders should consider alternatives. Chapter 3: Seven Steps to Implementing an Enrichment Cluster Program presents a number of creative and effective approaches to scheduling.

An additional issue related to scheduling has to do with time for staff development and sharing. There is a good deal of interest these days in faculties coming together as "communities of learners," but the actual implementation of this very good idea has frequently manifested itself in book discussion groups or discussions about local or national education issues. Such endeavors can be valuable, but some time devoted to brainstorming and sharing innovative solutions to real and present challenges will help a faculty develop a "can-do" attitude. The school's regular staff development agenda should include sessions that focus on facilitating enrichment clusters and sharing ideas. Scheduling time for staff development and discussions about the program, as well as an opportunity for sharing and celebrating successes and struggles, will pay off in terms of shared expertise, renewed enthusiasm, and the generation of creative ideas.

8. Suspend the customs of regular schooling. Many regulations and traditions guide schools and classrooms. We are not questioning the value of these traditions, but we want "cluster time" to be different from the regular school environment. Some of these differences have already been mentioned—cross-grade grouping by interests, a focus on products and services rather than acquisition of predetermined knowledge, and teaching that does not follow traditional lesson or unit plans. There are other customs that we want to avoid if enrichment clusters are to be qualitatively different from regular schooling. For example, group size may vary considerably from one cluster to another. One cluster may contain eight or 10 students, while across the hall a cluster of 40 students meets. The larger cluster might need two or more adult facilitators or simply a teacher who is at ease moving from one small group to another within the large cluster. Some clusters may need to be carried out in nonclassroom environments (e.g., a daycare or senior center, a local business office or theater, or outside on the school grounds). Because clusters are modeled after learning that takes place in the real world, the environment should fit the students and the cluster topic rather than forcing the students and topic to a particular environment. And even within regular classrooms, furniture and equipment should be rearranged to accommodate the task requirements. Although clusters usually last a designated number of weeks, some clusters may require more time. One cluster that developed a television production company that aired a weekly program on a local cable access channel lasted 6 years! New students joined the company as others moved on to high school, but the success, enjoyment, commitment of the facilitators, and ever-emerging professionalism on the parts of the students were the best reasons for enabling the cluster to continue for an extended period of time.

The goal of this guideline is to make the type of learning, the environment, and the entire atmosphere of enrichment clusters as unschoollike as possible. Such a goal is not a criticism of regular schooling as much as a way to enhance those things that make inductive learning a more natural chain of events in the high-end learning process.

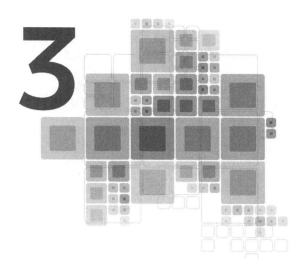

3

SEVEN STEPS TO IMPLEMENTING AN ENRICHMENT CLUSTER PROGRAM

Something that's good doesn't work by itself just to please you. You've got to make the damn thing work!

—Thomas Edison

In order to begin implementation, the school staff must decide who will organize the enrichment cluster program. We have seen successful programs coordinated by parent volunteers, principals, and enrichment specialists. We have found, though, that a good way to encourage the entire school family to become involved is to develop a schoolwide enrichment team consisting of teachers, parents, administrators, staff, and even students. A brief set of guidelines for forming an enrichment team can be found in *The Schoolwide Enrichment Model* (Renzulli & Reis, 2014). Building a team helps foster feelings of ownership and encourages creative input from all stakeholders. Not all schools need to coordinate a cluster program in the same manner, but determining at the outset who is responsible for what aspects of the program will help ensure that it runs smoothly.

In our 20 years of working with teachers, parents, and administrators who implemented enrichment cluster programs, seven steps emerged as an efficient set of strategies for organizing and launching the program. Although most of the schools with which we were involved followed these steps sequentially, some schools may choose to pursue certain activities simultaneously. As the planning process unfolds, individuals or small groups of teachers may want to examine procedures outlined in Chapter 4: How to Develop Your Own Enrichment Cluster.

STEP 1: LEARN ABOUT THE INTERESTS OF STUDENTS AND STAFF MEMBERS

Many teachers struggle to extend a degree of choice to students in their classrooms within the limits of the curriculum. In many classrooms, all students perform the same activities despite having different interests and talents. Enrichment clusters offer opportunities to regularly explore interests and develop talents outside the confines of a scripted curriculum. Our research (described briefly in Chapter 6: Research Underlying the Enrichment Cluster Program) indicates that grouping students by interest may be more effective than traditional grouping patterns in producing or delivering meaningful products or services. Within the cluster, choice continues to exist and follows student strengths, styles, and preferences. Everyone in a newspaper cluster works on the production of the newspaper, but different students may select different roles, such as layout designer, editor, photographer, or features writer.

When implementing an enrichment cluster program, leaders must first learn more about the interests and talents of students and staff (including all faculty, aides, nurses, counselors, custodians, and any other adult in the school). This information-gathering process encourages students and staff to consider their own individual strengths and interests and develops a pool of potential enrichment cluster topics. We have found that all adults associated with the school become much more excited about their work when they have the opportunity to facilitate a cluster on something that they love.

STUDENT INTERESTS

Cluster program leaders can use a variety of interest assessment instruments to identify present or potential student interests. For the elementary students in our original study, we used the survey "If I Ran the School" (Burns, 1992), which can be found in Appendix A. This instrument lists general fields of interest as well as specific areas within each field. Students select 10 topics that they might like to explore from the general areas of science, social studies and history, mathematics, art, and language arts. Within the science field, for example, students can choose from more specific topics such as stars and planets, reptiles, the human body, and rocks and minerals. Nowadays we suggest using Survey Monkey (http://www.surveymonkey.com) to collect these data electronically. We also suggest adding areas of local interest tied to specific focuses of the curriculum. For educators who use the Renzulli Learning System (http://www.renzullilearning.com), student interest data will be readily available.

In our research, we found that "If I Ran the School" works well with students in the first grade and above. However, students (especially primary grade students) who may not have been exposed to a broad variety of topics may not exhibit strong interests in specific areas. Instead, these students may be enthusiastic about everything. In such cases, we recommend using an age-appropriate interest assessment from a set of questionnaires entitled The Interest-A-Lyzer Family of Instruments (Renzulli, 1997). These questionnaires span particular grade groups (K–3, 4–8, 7–12) and can help young people take a more in-depth look at their present and potential interests. Whichever instruments you choose to use, we recommend that students complete them in school so that students and teachers have opportunities to discuss responses. (After these surveys have been used for assessing interests and determining possible cluster topics, they can be placed in the classroom for teachers to use as they engage in differentiation or curriculum compacting.) Although some teams may be tempted to skip this interest assessment process in an effort to get the program off the ground quickly, a little time spent helping students examine their interests will contribute greatly to the success of the enrichment cluster program.

Next, program leaders should tally the responses of these surveys across classrooms to get a general idea about the scope of student interests and determine the approximate number of clusters that might be offered in general curricular areas. High tallies for science topics, for example, will indicate that more science clusters should be offered. In several of our pilot programs, we identified the top 15 to 20 interest areas in a school, and then tried to match those student interests with staff, parent, and community talents. Figure 3.1 lists the top 20 interests from one elementary school.

ADULT INTERESTS

We developed an adult interest survey, "Inspiration" (Gentry & Renzulli, 1995), especially for use by potential facilitators (see Handout 3.1a: Inspiration Survey in Chapter 5: Staff Development and Program Evaluation). In this survey, adults consider their interests and talents by listing hobbies, affiliations, professional and personal experiences, and other personal choice options. The survey presents open-ended questions such as the following to stimulate thinking:

- "If you had no limits whatsoever, what would you like to do in your spare time?"

Student Interests	
1. Dinosaurs	11. Holidays
2. Calculators and Computers	12. Languages (e.g., Spanish, French, American Sign Language)
3. Cartoons	13. Drawing
4. Art Projects	14. Rocks and Minerals
5. Volcanoes and Earthquakes	15. Making New Toys
6. Monsters and Mysteries	16. Stars and Planets
7. Math Games and Puzzles	17. Outer Space, Astronauts, and Rockets
8. Life in the Ocean	18. Reptiles
9. Animals and Their Homes	19. Chemistry and Experiments
10. Magic	20. Castles and Knights

FIGURE 3.1. Top 20 student interests as determined by schoolwide interest assessment.

- "Describe the one thing that you feel has been your most creative contribution to teaching."
- "What cause would you take up if you had the time?"

Faculty and staff can complete the survey at a faculty meeting in less than 15 minutes, or take it home if they want time to reflect on their responses. Program leaders should consider having all faculty and staff members and potential community volunteers complete and return the survey to them. "Inspiration" can be especially helpful in the beginning phases of implementing an enrichment cluster program, when potential facilitators may not have ideas about what they want to offer students.

STEP 2: SET UP A WALL CHART

Setting up a wall chart is an important part of implementing a successful enrichment cluster program. The chart helps program leaders and potential facilitators organize student interests into major disciplines and then begin outlining possible clusters that would meet those interests. Figure 3.2 presents a sample wall chart, but each school's wall chart will be different. The wall chart should begin with general areas of knowledge listed on the left side as in Figure 3.2. These areas will change from school to school. For example, some schools might combine mathematics, computers, and technology into a single general area of knowledge,

General Interest Areas	Specific Examples of Clusters
Language Arts, Literature, and the Humanities	The Young Authors' Guild The Poets' Workshop The African American Literary Society The Investigative Journalism Group The Quarterly Review of Children's Literature Graphic Novel Society
Physical and Life Sciences	The Save the Dolphins Society The Physical Science Research Institute The Mansfield Environmental Protection Agency The Experimental Robotics Team
The Arts	The Electronic Music Research Institute The Visual Artists' Workshops The Meriden Theater Company The Native American Dance Institute The Video Production Company The Young Musicians' Ensemble The Photographers' Guild Digital Maestros
Social Sciences	The Hispanic Cultural Awareness Association The Junior Historical Society The Social Science Research Team The Torrington Geographic Society The Creative Cartographers' Guild Cache Chasers
Mathematics	The Math Materials Publication Company The Math Mentors' Association The Female Mathematicians' Support Group The Mathematics Competitions League The Math Puzzle Challenge Quarterly
Technology	Dazzling Designs Publishing House Google Lit Trippers iPad Orchestra The Computer Games Production Company The Computer Literacy Assistance Association The Creative Software Society The Desktop Publishing Company App Builders Workshop Programming Posse
Physical Education and Wellness	The Experimental Games Research Team The Physiology of Sport Study Group The Physical Fitness Support Group The Institute for the Study of Multicultural Recreation Nutrition and Exercise Community Outreach
Family and Consumer Sciences	Creative Furniture Design Company The Architecture for Learning Research Team The Experimental Dietary Group The Future Fashion Research Institute The Childcare Assistance Group

FIGURE 3.2. Sample wall chart.

and other schools may want to separate the arts into the visual and performing arts. Furthermore, a general area called Interdisciplinary Studies might combine the arts and the sciences in one school and math and social studies in another. Organizing interests under general areas of knowledge helps facilitators and program leaders focus on how possible cluster topics fit into the scholarly domains of knowledge. This focus leads toward more academic rigor as leaders go about the process of organizing and developing clusters. There are no hard and fast rules about setting up the left side of the wall chart, but this approach to planning will help accommodate the diverse interests of all students. It is not a good idea to list themes (e.g., conflict, power, change, revolution, relationships) or topics (e.g., architecture, transportation, holidays, animals) on the left side of the chart. A thematic approach to curriculum might work in other venues, but the focus of enrichment clusters is on the content and methods of practicing professionals in real-world situations; the starting point should be the ways in which knowledge is organized in the adult world.

The results of the students' interest surveys (including the number of students who checked the respective items on "If I Ran the School" or another survey) can be classified and recorded on the left side of the chart to get an estimate of the number of clusters that might be developed for each general area of knowledge. Higher frequencies in certain areas indicate that program leaders should prepare for more clusters to meet potential student demand. Staff members can then begin to fill in possible enrichment clusters that they could offer that would fit the general areas of knowledge.

A SPECIAL NOTE ABOUT CRAFTS AND HOBBIES

Although crafts and hobbies hold great value, we must emphasize the importance of academic and artistic rigor in clusters. In several of the districts and schools that implemented clusters as part of our research, some parents expressed concerns about taking time away from serious schooling in order to work on activities that students enjoy. These parents carefully read cluster descriptions that were sent home and questioned any cluster that did not seem academically challenging. Staff members who want to offer clusters in areas such as anime, cooking, cake decorating, line dancing, or quilting should brainstorm ways that they can professionalize aspects of the craft and how they can raise the level of challenge and rigor. A teacher with a lifelong interest in quilting used this craft as a vehicle for documenting local history, and students in a cluster on cooking conducted research using taste tests and prepared illustrated cookbooks for special occasions and activities. Children could turn art and craft clusters into small businesses (e.g., greeting card companies, key chain and decorative pin companies) and in the process learn a great deal about purchasing, accounting, marketing, advertising, sales, and other aspects of microeconomics. By focusing on what professionals do in particular areas and what possible future career options might be, facilitators can escalate the level of challenge in a cluster and ensure academic rigor.

STEP 3: CREATE A SCHEDULE

Before beginning an enrichment cluster program (and, if possible, before the school year begins), program leaders must identify a specific time within the school week for cluster activities. To be successful and valued, clusters should not have to compete for time with pull-out programs, special programs, or teacher planning time. They should have their own place within the school week schedule, just like other subjects and activities that are valued and part of the school program. Furthermore, in order to keep the focus on talent development, all students should be involved in enrichment clusters. No students should be excluded from pursuing their interests because of scheduling conflicts with physical education, remedial reading programs, band, chorus, or other special programs. Also, as we have discussed, the activities that take place within clusters are different from other activities in the school and should be defined by a distinct time block. This time should not be used as a catch-all for school photos, standardized tests, and other miscellaneous activities, but should be designated and used for enrichment clusters. If enrichment cluster time is lumped with other activities, students and staff will learn that the school leaders do not value enrichment.

If an enrichment cluster program will be implemented within an existing schedule after the school year has begun, program leaders must obtain staff input at every step. Staff participation in the planning process helps earn staff member support and contributes to the success of the program. The faculty and staff should make decisions about the following items:

- length of the cluster blocks (8 or more weeks recommended),
- number of blocks per year (at least one recommended),
- length of each cluster session (at least 75 minutes recommended), and
- day(s) of week and the time of day (set based on school schedule; consensus of staff recommended).

Examples of successful enrichment cluster schedules appear in Table 3.1 (a period exchange schedule), Table 3.2 (a half-day schedule), and Table 3.3 (a double-period rotating schedule). In addition, an "assembly" schedule that shortens class periods by an equal number of minutes is popular with middle schools and also works in elementary schools. The number of minutes that the staff chooses to reallocate to develop a cluster time block is an individual school decision, but we

TABLE 3.1
PERIOD EXCHANGE SCHEDULE

	MONDAY	TUESDAY	WEDNESDAY	THURSDAY	FRIDAY
WEEK 1 ETC.	Enrichment Clusters Math Language Arts Social Studies Etc.	Reading Enrichment Clusters Language Arts Social Studies Etc.	Reading Math Enrichment Clusters Social Studies Etc.	Reading Math Language Arts Enrichment Clusters Etc.	Reading Math Language Arts Social Studies Enrichment Clusters

TABLE 3.2
HALF-DAY SCHEDULE

	MONDAY	TUESDAY	WEDNESDAY	THURSDAY	FRIDAY
WEEK 1	Reading Math Language Arts Social Studies Etc.	Reading Math Language Arts Social Studies Etc.	Enrichment Clusters Reading Etc.	Reading Math Language Arts Social Studies Etc.	Reading Math Language Arts Social Studies Etc.
WEEK 2	Reading Math Language Arts Social Studies Etc.	Reading Math Language Arts Social Studies Etc.	Enrichment Clusters Math Etc.	Reading Math Language Arts Social Studies Etc.	Reading Math Language Arts Social Studies Etc.
WEEK 3	Reading Math Language Arts Social Studies Etc.	Reading Math Language Arts Social Studies Etc.	Enrichment Clusters Language Arts Etc.	Reading Math Language Arts Social Studies Etc.	Reading Math Language Arts Social Studies Etc.
WEEK 4 ETC.	Reading Math Language Arts Social Studies Etc.	Reading Math Language Arts Social Studies Etc.	Enrichment Clusters Social Studies Etc.	Reading Math Language Arts Social Studies Etc.	Reading Math Language Arts Social Studies Etc.

TABLE 3.3
DOUBLE-PERIOD ROTATING SCHEDULE

	MONDAY	TUESDAY	WEDNESDAY	THURSDAY	FRIDAY
WEEK 1	Enrichment Clusters Language Arts Social Studies Etc.	Reading Math Language Arts Social Studies Etc.	Reading Math Language Arts Social Studies Etc.	Reading Math Language Arts Social Studies Etc.	Reading Math Language Arts Social Studies Etc.
WEEK 2	Reading Math Enrichment Clusters Etc.	Reading Math Language Arts Social Studies Etc.	Reading Math Language Arts Social Studies Etc.	Reading Math Language Arts Social Studies Etc.	Reading Math Language Arts Social Studies Etc.
WEEK 3	Reading Math Language Arts Social Studies Etc.	Enrichment Clusters Language Arts Social Studies Etc.	Reading Math Language Arts Social Studies Etc.	Reading Math Language Arts Social Studies Etc.	Reading Math Language Arts Social Studies Etc.
WEEK 4	Reading Math Language Arts Social Studies Etc.	Reading Math Enrichment Clusters Etc.	Reading Math Language Arts Social Studies Etc.	Reading Math Language Arts Social Studies Etc.	Reading Math Language Arts Social Studies Etc.
WEEK 5	Reading Math Language Arts Social Studies Etc.	Reading Math Language Arts Social Studies Etc.	Enrichment Clusters Language Arts Social Studies Etc.	Reading Math Language Arts Social Studies Etc.	Reading Math Language Arts Social Studies Etc.
WEEK 6	Reading Math Language Arts Social Studies Etc.	Reading Math Language Arts Social Studies Etc.	Enrichment Clusters Language Arts Social Studies Etc.	Reading Math Language Arts Social Studies Etc.	Reading Math Language Arts Social Studies Etc.
WEEK 7	Reading Math Language Arts Social Studies Etc.	Reading Math Language Arts Social Studies Etc.	Reading Math Language Arts Social Studies Etc.	Enrichment Clusters Language Arts Social Studies Etc.	Reading Math Language Arts Social Studies Etc.
WEEK 8 ETC.	Reading Math Language Arts Social Studies Etc.	Reading Math Language Arts Social Studies Etc.	Reading Math Language Arts Social Studies Etc.	Enrichment Clusters Language Arts Social Studies Etc.	Reading Math Language Arts Social Studies Etc.

recommend that cluster sessions last at least 75 minutes, with at least 90 minutes being best, and that clusters meet at least weekly.

LENGTH OF CLUSTER BLOCKS

The length of the cluster blocks can vary, but we have found that a minimum of 8 weeks is necessary to achieve in-depth involvement and high-quality products or services. Most schools planned clusters in 8- to 12-week time blocks, with several weeks between cluster blocks set aside for reflection, evaluation, and planning for the next set of clusters. Initial cluster blocks or a pilot series can be shorter. A 4–6 week pilot block in the fall lets students and teachers familiarize themselves with the cluster philosophy and routine and gives leaders a chance to evaluate the success of the program and resolve any conflicts.

School involvement in state or national talent development programs can also guide cluster block planning. Some schools have used the enrichment cluster program to allow students to participate in programs such as Invention Convention, Destination Imagination, Math League, The International Future Problem Solving Program, various science and technology competitions, and the National History Day Competition. These programs are naturals for meeting the requirements of enrichment clusters, and their yearlong or seasonal time frames can be taken into consideration when scheduling enrichment cluster blocks.

NUMBER OF BLOCKS PER YEAR

The length of cluster blocks will determine the number that can fit into the school year. Typical patterns have been three 8-week blocks or two 10–12 week blocks, but each enrichment team should examine its own scheduling options and make adjustments accordingly. Furthermore, not all clusters need to conform to the same time frames. An ongoing cluster such as a school newspaper, yearbook, or weekly school news video program may continue throughout the year, while other clusters are carried out on a rotation basis. Enrichment clusters are, by their very nature, a deviation from traditional ways of teaching and learning and should not fall into a one-size-fits-all pattern of organization. Some clusters take more time than others because of the nature of the tasks and the level of the material being pursued. Flexibility in scheduling is as important as flexibility in teaching and learning processes. As is always the case with new initiatives, scheduling should be approached on an experimental basis, and creative problem solving should be a hallmark of the process of developing a sustainable program.

THE LENGTH OF EACH CLUSTER SESSION

An enrichment cluster is a different environment, freeing students from the traditional role of being "under instruction." In clusters, individuals and small groups of students should work independently and at their own pace, and many activities will not have neat beginning and ending targets. As a result, enrichment clusters will benefit from a longer time period than the common 45-minute class period.

In our pilot schools and subsequent work with enrichment cluster programs, teachers have found that one hour was the absolute minimum time needed for a fruitful cluster session. Shorter periods tended to be rushed and did not provide adequate time to accomplish successful hands-on exploration and product development. In examining different clusters, we found that a double class period of about 90 minutes (the equivalent of two regularly scheduled class periods) allows enough time for effective engagement in cluster activities. Because the work pursued in clusters is different from the more routine ways in which traditional instruction is scheduled and because clusters ordinarily do not meet every day, it takes students time to settle down and to catch up with the work they did in previous sessions. In one pilot site, clusters met for 2 hours each week, and this longer time period allowed for much more in-depth learning to take place.

THE DAY(S) OF THE WEEK AND THE TIME OF DAY

Based on experiences in pilot schools, we recommend that clusters meet at least once a week in order to maintain a continuity of activities. If students have to wait 2 weeks between projects, interest and recall wane. (However, there are exceptions: Some pilot schools chose to follow the first cluster session with a 2–3-week break. This break allowed facilitators to consider initial discussions with students and gather needed materials.) The day of the week and time of day for enrichment clusters depends upon school needs and preferences. Some enrichment teams have scheduled clusters on Fridays as an exciting end to the week; others prefer to break up routine with cluster activities midweek.

In our work with schools, we have found a variety of schedules that were successful. In one program, clusters met for an hour and 15 minutes in the afternoon each week. Teachers at another site did not want clusters to meet at the end of the day because they found that students needed time after each cluster session to share what happened in their clusters with classmates in their regular classes. Clusters in this school met midweek in the morning, with student returning to class with enough time before lunch to allow them to discuss their clusters with others. Many middle and high schools have lunch activity periods, and some chose to devote one of these periods each week to enrichment clusters. If schools already use lunch activity periods to support extracurricular activities such as drama club, yearbook, school newspaper, Destination Imagination, Science Olympiad, or Future Problem Solving, they then need only to develop other clusters to meet all student and staff interests.

Scheduling is one of the biggest challenges that schools face, and it is even more challenging when it requires inserting a new component into the school week. If schools value the kind of high-end learning that is the goal of enrichment clusters, and if they use their collective creative problem-solving skills, they can meet the scheduling challenge. As one teacher put it, "If we can put the entire Library of Congress on a few computer chips, surely we can be creative enough to make a few changes in the schedule!" Once clusters have become part of the schedule, they are part of the expected school week. The challenge comes only in the first year or two when they are added. After a few years, no one will question why clusters are in the schedule any more than they question reading, art, or lunch.

STEP 4: LOCATE PEOPLE TO FACILITATE CLUSTERS

Locating people to facilitate clusters can be as simple or involved as needed for each school situation. Many schools use only staff and a few parent volunteers to facilitate clusters, and the program works wonderfully. Other programs extended a wider reach with much success. Our pilot sites found volunteers to facilitate clusters from many different sources, including teachers and school staff, parents, community volunteers, and college students (see Figure 3.3). The ways in which the community can be involved will depend on the amount of help available for implementing the program. The more involved everyone is in making decisions and implementing the program, the greater the ownership of the program and the better the chance of success.

FACILITATORS FROM THE SCHOOL TEACHERS

The first and obvious place to look for people to facilitate clusters is in school. In our pilot programs, we distributed lists of top student interests at staff meetings. Several teachers organized their clusters based on these student interests, and we encouraged teachers to team up with a friend or other staff member, which often makes the process even more enjoyable.

In addition, the "Inspiration" survey may reveal talents, interests, or hobbies that could become cluster topics. After reviewing the results of the survey, program leaders can ask teachers with special interests and talents to consider facilitating a cluster. At one of the pilot schools, a teacher who completed the survey indicated that she enjoyed playing in a handbell choir at her church, but did not feel comfortable organizing a handbell cluster. With some encouragement, she teamed up

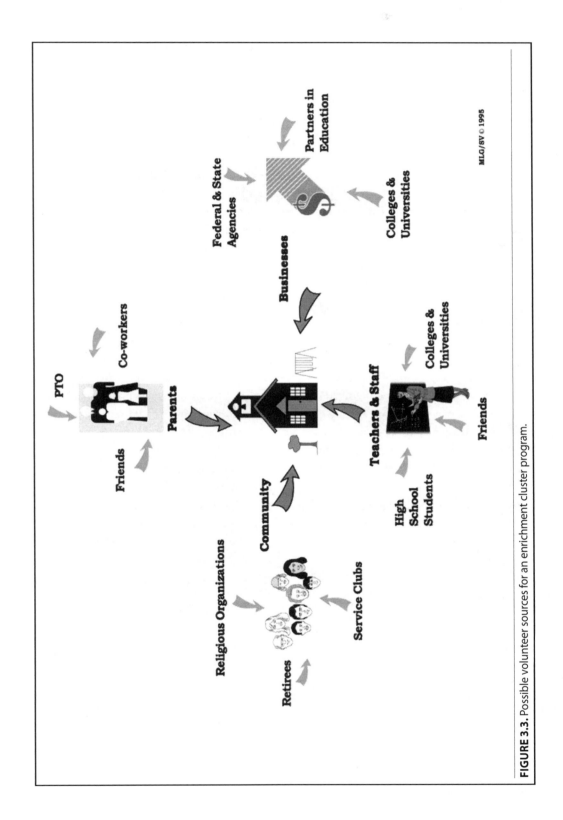

FIGURE 3.3. Possible volunteer sources for an enrichment cluster program.

with the school nurse and the choir director to facilitate The Chimers: A Handbell Choir.

At first, teachers may believe they must only offer cluster topics that are "academic" or related to the curriculum. Although these topics may certainly be the focus of enrichment clusters, teachers should feel free to choose topics of personal interest to them. What we have learned in working with enrichment clusters is that any topic can be academically rigorous, even if at first blush it does not appear to be related to the district or state curriculum. All clusters involve advanced content, advanced resources, and authentic methods, and just about any topic if approached in a true enrichment cluster fashion has an rigorous, interesting, professional angle, from skateboarding (e.g., designing a park) to game development (e.g., creating the next commercial app or game for smartphones). The magic of enrichment clusters is in the application of learning to real-world problems—an area frequently overlooked in traditional academics.

SUPPORT STAFF

Although teachers may be the most obvious choice to facilitate enrichment clusters, support staff can provide a wealth of resources for a cluster program. Successful clusters involve everyone in the school, and all adults in a school should be encouraged to become involved in clusters. (Because support staff may not attend faculty meetings, program leaders should approach them individually to introduce them to the program.) We found exceptional cluster activities built around the talents and interests of instructional assistants, secretaries, custodians, nurses, special education teachers, counselors, school psychologists, principals, and superintendents. A school secretary who had been a painter for 35 years and who had won several awards for her watercolors organized a successful cluster called Young Artists. A custodian organized a cluster for middle school students on how the building works. The cluster students developed diagrams detailing how the school works from the inside out to share with interested classes. This cluster involved learning how to read blueprints and engineering diagrams, and they used resource materials that brought them into contact with architecture, heating and ventilation, building codes, and landscape planning. Similarly, a school nurse guided students through advanced investigations in anatomy and physiology. Students presented health-related messages to others in the school and prepared an exhibit of posters and brochures on healthy living that they displayed at a local shopping mall. The students helped interested people measure their pulse, blood pressure, and cholesterol levels. Several students indicated that the work they carried out in this cluster motivated them to think about careers in medicine and health-related fields.

FACILITATORS FROM THE COMMUNITY

Often there is a good deal of overlap between staff and student interests, but there will always be areas of student interest not covered by school staff interests. Parents and community volunteers may fill these gaps and be able to provide resources, materials, and authenticity within a specific profession or topic that can be extremely exciting and motivating to students and adults as well. We suggest three steps for procuring volunteers not affiliated with the school:

1. **Create a network.** Ask teachers, staff, parents, and others for suggestions; check local businesses, retirement communities, agencies, professional and service organizations, leagues, and clubs. These sources will generate a good list of possibilities. You can even have a contest at a faculty meeting to see who recruits the most creative cluster facilitator from outside the faculty.

2. **Call prospective volunteers.** Describe the program briefly. If someone seems interested but does not want to commit to a full series, look for ways to accommodate his or her needs, such as being a guest speaker or hosting a field trip. Ask for suggestions from someone else in the field or organization who might be interested in organizing a cluster. Some of these contacts are the best leads for finding cluster facilitators.

3. **Meet with interested volunteers.** Discuss cluster philosophy in greater detail, provide literature on the program and school procedures, and answer questions. For volunteers outside the school, a personal contact is very important. Not only do the volunteer's abilities need to be assessed, but the volunteer will feel more comfortable after seeing the school, meeting the coordinator, and discussing the program. For obvious reasons, the importance of timelines and dependability also needs to be stressed when orientation is provided for new cluster facilitators.

Staff members who choose not to facilitate a cluster of their own may be paired with community volunteers to help with questions, assist with cluster activities and discipline, and, in the event of illness or absence, facilitate the cluster. Every effort should be made to allow staff to choose the cluster that they assist.

PARENTS

Parents are an often underutilized resource in schools. To involve parents in an enrichment cluster program, leaders should send letters home inviting parents to facilitate or help with a cluster. Program leaders can also contact parents through teachers, at PTA meetings, or through phone calls. Parents may be reluctant at first, and may be more inclined to become involved if they receive a list of ideas from which to choose. After being contacted by a pilot school enrichment team member, one parent expressed that she would love to assist in the program, but did not think she had any talents the school could use. When she received information about areas of student interests, she noted that some students were interested in math games and puzzles. Because of her own love for puzzles and mathematics, she decided to develop a cluster entitled The Mathematics and Puzzle Guild. Students explored different types of games and puzzles that they could create themselves. With the help of this parent, students developed their own puzzle books and board games to share with family and friends and for teachers to use in enrichment centers in their classrooms.

Another way to involve parents is to ask if they would be willing to assist with a cluster. Some parents may not be aware of their skills or talents or may not feel competent to teach. Assisting a facilitator with a cluster will introduce these parents to the program and to student-driven learning, and once they have some experience, they may feel more able to organize their own cluster.

Some parents who work may not be able to commit to helping with a full series of clusters, but they may still want to take part in the program. These parents may be able to help for a week or two, serve as guest speakers, assist with phone calls or computer activities, act as a substitute in case of illness, or provide transportation for cluster field trips. Cluster organizers should make it clear to parents that they are welcome at any time and that any input is valuable and appreciated.

COMMUNITY VOLUNTEERS

Many schools want to encourage more business and community involvement, and inviting members of the community into the enrichment cluster program is a means of making connections. Likewise, local businesses often have outreach programs, and business owners may volunteer employees to facilitate a cluster (especially if they know that a brochure describing the cluster and the facilitator is sent to a few hundred parents).

Our pilot school enrichment teams found a huge resource in the options for cluster volunteers from outside the school environment. These resources are unique to each community and depend upon the individuals and businesses within the community. A good place to begin is with suggestions from teachers and parents. Community volunteers are generally willing and eager to spend time for a good cause in a mentor role, but if they cannot, they may be able to suggest someone who can. From these contacts, schools can develop a network of possible names and ideas. If a specific profession based on student interests is needed, the phone book can also serve as a good resource. Public agencies are another great place to explore. Many park employees, youth services staff, police officers, and fire department workers are generally willing and able to spend time with students, and in many cases they have experience working with groups of children. In addition, volunteering to facilitate a cluster is often a win-win situation for both parties. In one of our pilot sites, a local park provided a biologist to facilitate a cluster on forest and wildlife biology. The students gained the benefit of firsthand experience with a wildlife biologist and the resources and materials that he brought, while the park benefited from the chance to set up some youth programs based on the biologist's experience with the cluster.

STUDENT TEACHERS, INTERNS, AND OLDER STUDENTS

Student teachers and interns can also be wonderful resources for organizing clusters. These students are usually eager to gain experience working with small groups of children, and they may have some background knowledge and interest in working with children. Students who attend nearby colleges or universities are another valuable resource, as they often need to fulfill a community service requirement for graduation. If they are in the field of education, they are required to spend time in classroom settings, and clusters provide valuable opportunities for these students to share their skills and talents with younger students while gaining experience for their own careers.

High school students can also facilitate clusters. The high school's enrichment teacher, honors class teachers, National Honor Society advisor, or guidance counselors may be able to provide referrals. Even in an elementary or middle school, older students can work with younger students under the guidance of an adult supervisor. (It is a good idea to pair these students with an adult on staff.)

A NOTE ABOUT NONSCHOOL STAFF

Involving volunteers, community members, and parents raises issues about certification and background checks. Different states have different guidelines, and different boards of education have different policies, so first schools need to determine their state laws and board policies. Depending on their state, schools may be able to treat this situation in the same manner as when noncertified staff (e.g., an aide or reading volunteer) works with students. Alternatively, schools may need to designate a certified staff member as a supervisor and have this person "float" between areas where volunteers are working with students. Program leaders need to make decisions about the certification issue before the program starts, and if the state or school system requires background checks for volunteers, schools will need to complete them before the program begins. In such cases, students in college and university education programs are a good resource, as they will have the necessary background checks in place.

STEP 5: PROVIDE ORIENTATION FOR FACILITATORS

Remembering their own experiences from school, community and parent facilitators may feel they need to "teach" a subject using a lecture format, worksheets, and traditional information transfer techniques. Even the most experienced teachers may initially want to continue the types of teaching methods that typically occur in their classrooms. Orienting the facilitators, therefore, is crucial to keeping clusters from becoming minicourses, theme units, or traditional teacher-directed experiences. Student-directed, hands-on activities and exploration require that facilitators make substantial changes in the ways they view teaching and the ways in which they guide activities in enrichment clusters.

Orientation for cluster facilitators serves two major goals. The first goal is to help facilitators gain an understanding of and appreciation for the differences between traditional teaching techniques and student-driven learning and teaching as defined in Chapters 1 and 2. This goal can be achieved by reviewing this material in small discussion groups, participating in Activity 1.1: Skills We Bring With Us (see Chapter 5: Staff Development and Program Evaluation), or reviewing examples on the enrichment cluster website (http://www.gifted.uconn.edu) or "Enrichment Cluster Exchange" Facebook page. Allowing future facilitators to observe effective clusters is also a very good way to orient them. Chapter 5: Staff Development and Program Evaluation presents additional activities designed to provide background knowledge about the program and stimulate teacher and community buy-in.

The second goal of orientation is to provide actual know-how for developing an authentic enrichment cluster. Chapter 4: How to Develop Your Own Enrichment Cluster offers a step-by-step guide for the process. Presentations by experienced cluster facilitators and examinations of cluster descriptions and the work of students in existing or completed clusters will also help facilitators gain practical tips for planning and guiding their own clusters.

Orientation should be ongoing. At the conclusion of each series of clusters, program leaders should schedule at least one meeting that focuses on sharing know-how and cluster experiences, addressing challenges and difficulties that may have occurred in the clusters, reviewing students' products, and exchanging ideas about possible topics and techniques for future clusters. They should review cluster feedback evaluation forms from students and from facilitators and use the data to improve the program. These discussions should call attention to how students engaged in high levels of inquiry and used advanced content. It is important for these debriefing sessions to be conducted in an atmosphere that strikes a thoughtful balance between reporting the positive things that individuals have done and examining ways to improve future clusters. A good way to approach this delicate balance is to ask everyone to write a statement for discussion that begins with the stem, "I would like to get your suggestions about ways in which I can . . ." These statements might focus on where to find advanced resources, ways of expanding options for student products, how to keep reluctant students engaged, possible audiences for student products or services, or how to apportion time among subgroups in the cluster. The general atmosphere should be one of continuous professional growth. *Creative Problem Solving* by Treffinger, Isaksen, and Dorval (2000) presents an excellent approach to the feedback and sharing process. The book provides the basics of Creative Problem Solving (CPS) as well as new advances in CPS that help make the process even more natural, flexible, and "user-friendly." (A summary of the CPS process can be downloaded from http://www.cpsb.com/resources/downloads/public/CPSVersion61B.pdf).

STEP 6: REGISTER STUDENTS FOR CLUSTERS THAT INTEREST THEM

A brochure of cluster descriptions and facilitator bios along with a registration form can help students choose and register for clusters, and students can complete registration in school or at home. If students will be taking the brochure home, program leaders should prepare a cover letter that explains to parents the program's goals and how they might help their child choose a cluster. At the middle and high school levels, it is better to have students register in school. However, schools should still keep parents informed by sending home updates about the clusters.

Effective registration is key to developing a smooth-running enrichment cluster program. Placing students in clusters with others who share their interest creates an exciting synergy. Ideally, program leaders should plan to offer one cluster for every 10 to 15 students, as space and personnel permit. Clusters can and will be smaller or larger, depending upon the number of interested students. In their descriptions, cluster facilitators should note the maximum and minimum number of students and the grade levels of the students they would be willing to accommodate in their clusters. For example, a theater cluster may need at least 15 students and be able to accommodate as many as 30 students because it requires so many diverse roles (designing sets, writing scripts, acting, directing, etc.). On the other hand, in a technology cluster, 15 students may be overwhelming due to space and equipment considerations. Finding a balance of students for the roles within the clusters contributes to the success of the clusters. By allowing facilitators to determine minimum and maximum numbers and grade levels, those who place students in the cluster have clear guidelines and those who facilitate have some control over the number of students they will guide.

When students register for clusters, they should choose three clusters without ranking them. Program leaders can then assign students to clusters and avoid student complaints about not being placed in a first-choice cluster. This is suggested because of a situation that occurred in a pilot series when students listed their top three choices in order of preference. Although the majority (85%) of the students were placed into their first-choice cluster, those who were not were disappointed. During subsequent cluster series, students simply chose three clusters in no order of preference, and this procedure yielded happier students and facilitators. When students register, they should know that they will probably not be placed in the same cluster as their best buddy just because they selected the same three clusters. Students should be encouraged and directed to sign up for clusters in which they really want to participate, not those that their friends choose.

Registration should take place at least one week before the clusters begin so that facilitators can be notified of the number of students in their cluster and can prepare. Occasionally clusters that receive only a few registrations are canceled, if the facilitator believes the cluster would not be successful with so few students. We found that clusters that had to be canceled often revolved around topics with which students were unfamiliar. To help increase students' interest in clusters with low registration, facilitators can conduct exciting introductory activities at an assembly or in individual classrooms. These introduction sessions usually increase registration when the cluster is offered again. If a cluster is canceled, that facilitator can help with other clusters. In one elementary school, a puppetry cluster originally designed for 10 students was the most popular cluster choice. Forty students signed up for the cluster. Two other clusters had no students select them. These clusters were canceled, and the facilitators agreed to help out in the puppetry cluster, which was expanded to include 30 students in two neighboring classrooms. The original facilitator provided instruction and moved between classrooms, and the other adults helped individual students.

Actual placement in clusters may be organized in different ways. As students complete and return their cluster selection forms, program leaders place them in one of their cluster choices. When a cluster "fills," it is closed. With a minimum of three choices, there are sufficient options to ensure that all students are placed, and by not ranking them, students are more satisfied that they received one of their choices. Enrichment team members have flexibility to review students' choices and complete course rosters according to expressed wishes of the students. On occasions with wildly popular clusters, we have opened a second section to accommodate student enrollment.

Alternatively, students can take registration forms home to consider and discuss with parents, but complete them during a specified time in their classrooms at school. This method facilitates immediate and complete response to the registration process, as there is no wait for paperwork from home. It also reduces the influence of parents who may want to choose a cluster for their child (often in a perceived area of weakness, not of strength).

As program leaders register students, they will want to keep several considerations in mind:

- Is there a good cross-representation of ages, gender, and abilities? A span of three grade levels is ideal, although four grade levels will work in many cases. Age balance is also important. A cluster with 15 first graders and one fifth grader might need to be reconsidered. The fifth grader may want to select another cluster that will be appropriately challenging. When placing primary students, it is a good idea to include at least two children from the same class so that they feel comfortable. Although facilitators establish age ranges for their clusters, program leaders should maintain some flexibility for placing special needs or younger students.
- Is the student-to-teacher ratio satisfactory?
- Will extra adult supervision or help be needed?
- Are the students' choices appropriate for their interests and abilities?

In one of the pilot sites, some students with special needs had specific requirements that could not be met in some clusters. Their special education teachers monitored their selections to ensure appropriate placement. In another site, a mathematically talented student who was achieving several grades above his chronological level selected a math cluster that would have provided little or no challenge. The cluster facilitator contacted the student to explain the content, and the student chose another, more challenging alternative. Because students select their clusters based on interest, it is rare that they are unhappy with their assigned cluster, but it does sometimes occur. If students decide they don't like their assigned cluster, several options exist:

- Do nothing. Explain to the student that the program is just beginning and that you'll check back in a couple of weeks to see if there is still a problem. Ninety percent of complaints disappear with this approach, as many complaints concern who is in the cluster, not what the cluster is about.
- Reassign the student to another cluster.
- Assign the student to a scheduled introductory cluster activity so he or she can get a taste of what the cluster will be about.
- Have the student remain in the cluster until the end of the series.

At one school, a student told his mother he was unhappy in his cluster, Young Voices Ensemble. She contacted the school, and program leaders offered to reassign him. She decided it would be better to wait one more week to see if her son would warm up to the cluster. It turned out that the student was just a little shy and needed more time to feel comfortable on stage. He stuck it out, earned a lead role in the musical, and ended up loving his cluster. We recommend trying to keep students involved in the cluster they choose and, whenever possible, providing the individual support and counseling necessary to help them resolve any problems that may occur.

Finally, after collecting registration forms from students and assigning them to clusters, we recommend establishing a database of information in order to generate three lists:

1. class lists for the homeroom teachers (so they know where their students are going),
2. class lists for the cluster facilitator, and
3. class lists for the office (in case a student must be contacted during cluster time).

We also suggest generating name tags so that facilitators can immediately call students by their names. With the cluster name and room number also printed on their tag, lost students can easily be redirected by staff members or older students.

STEP 7: CELEBRATE YOUR SUCCESS

Because they are so widely popular with students and staff, successful enrichment clusters are easy to celebrate, and they provide an almost unending source of material for public relations endeavors. Recognizing student and facilitator efforts is one of the best ways to call attention to the student products and services developed as a result of enrichment cluster activities. Some schools use display cases near the office to showcase cluster products. Alongside the sports trophy case near the office, where all visitors and students will see them, an "Academic Trophy Case" or a "Cluster Fair Showcase" can display exemplary cluster products. Schools can invite newspaper reporters to write feature articles about cluster activities and the unique products and services that emerge. Community members can attend product fairs that showcase all the products of enrichment clusters. One coordinator showcased his cluster program during the district's learning fair. It was so successful that the clusters became the centerpiece in this annual event. In one pilot school, some clusters pooled their efforts and produced a show to raise money for iPads for the school. By going public with the outcomes of the cluster program, schools can generate community support, school pride, and public awareness that may lead to future community involvement.

Newsletter	School TV	TV report
Banner behind airplane	National TV	Kids' show
Slideshow	News/Magazine article	District cable outlet
Reception	PTA meeting	Billboard
Banquet	Product rap for YouTube	Video
Open house	Photo album	School assembly
Invite a news reporter	Letters to celebrities	Brochure
Invite a school board member	Breakfast celebration	Scholastic Network
Who's Who directory	Service vendor fair	Talent fair
Portfolio recognition	Portfolio certificates	Programs at hospitals
Website	Make a CD	Board of Education
Glogster	Displays at school	Historical society
Share at conferences	Displays at malls	Programs for service clubs
Programs at retirement homes	Newspapers	High school
"Parade of Products"	Facebook	University groups

FIGURE 3.4. Possible outlets for cluster celebration.

In a staff development session dealing with implementing enrichment clusters at one of our pilot sites, a group of teachers, staff, parents, and community volunteers became so excited about the idea of celebrating success that they brainstormed a list of possibilities. The options are endless. Figure 3.4 lists some of their ideas.

Program leaders may choose to hold an awards ceremony to give students certificates of achievement. By recognizing students' accomplishments, schools can build upon the students' excitement and enthusiasm, which will transfer over to the general classroom. Thanking all cluster facilitators and volunteers is an equally important task. Schools can send out thank-you notes or certificates, present certificates of appreciation at a schoolwide assembly or other event, highlight efforts in the school newspaper, or combine different venues for expressing thanks.

For 2 years at Confratute, a summer conference for educators interested in gifted education and talent development held at the University of Connecticut, we have asked in our advanced enrichment cluster strand—developed for veteran enrichment cluster program coordinators—for their best advice to those who are beginning an enrichment cluster program. They suggest having a diverse enrichment team, with members from every grade level; setting aside networking and planning time to help get things up and running; keeping a sense of humor; and having all members of the educational community stress the importance of the program.

Relax, everything will be fine! Chevonne from Plano, TX, said, "Clusters are a learning experience for the kids and for us as educators. Before I began my first cluster I was so nervous that I wouldn't do the 'right thing.' I soon learned that there is no 'right thing' because every cluster group is unique, and that was a freeing feeling. Have fun with the kids. You won't be disappointed!" To connect with other educators who are clustering, be sure join the Enrichment Cluster Exchange on Facebook.

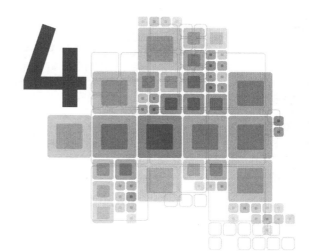

HOW TO DEVELOP YOUR OWN ENRICHMENT CLUSTER

The best classroom is where the teacher isn't.

—Jean Piaget

Developing an authentic enrichment cluster depends on an understanding of the goals of student-driven learning and of the differences between deductive and inductive learning. As you begin the process of developing your own cluster, you should keep the following four goals in mind:

1. Reverse the teaching equation. Your role in planning and facilitating an enrichment cluster is very different from traditional teaching. The more direct teaching you do in the cluster, the less likely you will be to turn the responsibility for creative and investigative activity over to the students. Although various planned start-up activities may be part of a cluster, too much planning on your part will push the cluster toward deductive rather than inductive teaching and learning. The absence of traditional unit and lesson planning prior to starting your work with students will undoubtedly cause some anxiety, but this anxiety is a healthy part of changing your orientation toward effective inductive teaching. Becoming comfortable in this type of learning environment will take a little time and direct experience facilitating a cluster. We might even go so far as to say that being too comfortable immediately could indicate that excessive control and routine has crept into a situation that should be more exploratory and flexible.

2. Reverse the role of students. For the sake of convenience, we have used the word "student" throughout this book. However, it is important that you transform the way you view young people in enrichment clusters. If you view young people as students only, you might think that your major responsibility is to teach them. If you are to alter your role from instructor to coach, mentor, referral agent, general contractor, or guide on the side, you must see students as potential young professionals. Young people working on an original piece of historical research, creative writing, journalism, or play production become young historians, authors, journalists, etc. This change in how you view students is important because it brings with it a different set of expectations for what students do and how you help them. Instead of teaching lessons, you will begin to think about how to help a young poet get his or her work published, how to get the shopping mall manager to allow space for a display of models of your town's historically significant buildings, and how to engineer a presentation by young environmentalists to the state wildlife commission.

3. Remember that each enrichment cluster is unique. As long as the guidelines for inductive teaching are followed, there is not a right or wrong way to plan and facilitate an enrichment cluster. Differences in interests, personalities, and styles between cluster facilitators are assets that contribute to the uniqueness of this type of learning. Even if you teach the same cluster on two or three different occasions, each rendition of the cluster should and will emerge as a unique entity. Although we offered guidelines for what defines enrichment clusters and discussed how to plan them in Chapter 2: What Is an Enrichment Cluster?, your involvement as a cluster planner and facilitator is, in and of itself, the best training for a type of teaching that purposefully differs from the models that attempt to standardize what teachers do. In this regard, you should view yourself as a work in progress. Inductive teaching is a more natural and, in many ways, easier process than structured teaching, but it also involves breaking some old habits based on traditional teacher roles. You will find that a little experience in an inductive learning environment will help you hone the skills that will eventually become a very natural part of your teaching repertoire both in clusters and in your classroom.

4. When in doubt, look outward! Because you are striving for a different brand of teaching and learning in enrichment clusters and because clusters are modeled after real-world situations, it is a good idea to examine nonclassroom conditions for models of planning and teaching and patterns of organization. An athletic coach, the advisor for the drama club or school newspaper, or a 4-H Club leader are excellent role models for enrichment cluster facilitators. Similarly, tasks and organizational patterns should resemble the activities that take place in a small business, a social service agency, a theater production company, or any laboratory that must generate real products and services. Your enrichment cluster will be most successful if the learning environment is as different as possible from that of a traditional classroom.

GUIDELINES FOR DEVELOPING AN ENRICHMENT CLUSTER

1. Select a topic. Your first enrichment cluster should be based on a topic in which you have a strong interest. Review your responses to the "Inspiration" survey and make a list of topics in which you are especially fascinated. Reflect on your choices, discuss your list with colleagues (there may be possibilities for collaboration), and rank the topics so that you can decide on the focus of your first enrichment cluster. Keep and add to the list and refer to it when choosing subsequent cluster topics. Some teachers at our pilot sites told us that there were dozens of topics they wanted to explore, while others had to do a bit of searching and exploring to develop a list. Some teachers have felt more comfortable teaming up with a colleague or community member with expertise in a particular topic or area of study. Our experience has also shown that once you become involved in this type of teaching, you will begin to examine various experiences with an eye toward how they might make possible cluster topics.

2. Examine key questions. Enrichment clusters are always developed around the six key questions listed in Figure 4.1. The questions do not need to be answered immediately, sequentially, or comprehensively at this stage of planning, but they should always be kept in mind as you follow the guidelines for cluster planning. Your examination of the key questions provides an orientation to the topic rather than definitive answers that you will then present to your students. As your cluster develops, early discussions with students should be geared toward leading them through the same set of questions and allowing them to reach their own conclusions about the activities, resources, and products that professionals pursue in particular areas of study. The introductory activities that you will develop for students should be designed to lead them through these questions and to discover for themselves the essential concerns that guide the work of practicing professionals in various fields. If you have all the answers before the cluster begins, the excitement of pure inquiry on the parts of the students will be lost.

3. Explore key questions. In many cases the answers to the key questions are common knowledge or common sense, but for purposes of clarification, we will discuss some of the ways that you can address the questions yourself and how you can guide your students through the questions as the cluster gets underway. The first and most obvious way to find out about the work of a professional is to find someone in a particular profession with whom you can talk. A brief interview with

1. What do people with an interest in this topic or area of study do?
2. What products do they create and/or what services do they provide?
3. What methods do they use to carry out their work?
4. What resources and materials are needed to produce high-quality products and services?
5. How and with whom do they communicate the results of their work?
6. What steps need to be taken to have an impact on intended audiences?

FIGURE 4.1. Key questions for developing enrichment clusters.

a cartoonist, a landscape architect, a fashion designer, or someone who works for the state environmental protection agency will give you the lay of the land and some recommended resources. When talking with professionals, keep in mind that you want to learn what they routinely do in their jobs, how they do it, and what they produce.

A word of caution: We have found that some professionals, whether working with teachers or students, gravitate toward a didactic mode that focuses more on dispensing facts rather than on the methodology and products associated with their area of specialization. A historian once told us that young people "couldn't do real historical research." You can imagine his surprise when a group of upper-elementary students produced an award-winning documentary that revealed previously unreported facts about a turn-of-the-century strike at a local factory.

Conveniently, almost all professions are organized into societies and associations. A quick Internet search will lead you to mountains of resources about these organizations. Just a quick search for "professional associations" shows approximately three million that cover almost every imaginable field of study. We went to the Association of Professional Genealogists website (http://www.apgen.org) and found a treasure trove of resources on the many different roles that people fill in the field (e.g., researchers, archivists, historians), state and national conferences, newsletters, publications that report findings, books on genealogical research methods, places where family records can be found, a listing of local chapters, and a directory of members by state. Individuals found on association membership lists can be valuable resources as speakers, mentors, or sources of local records. They might even be considered as a facilitator or cofacilitator of an enrichment cluster or a mentor to an individual or small group of students. By conducting an Internet search for genealogists in Connecticut, we found the names, addresses, and phone numbers of 13 professional genealogists in our state, one of whom lives less than five miles from our office.

A visit to the Genealogical Publishing Company website yielded an even more extensive list of potential resources—more than 2,000 titles. Librarians and college bookstores can also help locate methodological resource books. How-to books not only orient you (and students) in a field and provide information about how students can do authentic research, but will also give you ideas for specific studies,

special equipment or materials you might need, sources of data, newsletters or other places where research results might be published, or conferences that might offer opportunities for student presentations. Sharing examples with students of both typical and unusual products that might result from the cluster topic is also a good way to deal with key questions 1, 2, and 5.

Continuing with the genealogy example, some students might want to do written genealogical reports of their family history or the history of a famous individual, but others might consider a graphic representation of a family tree, a pictorial display board, a computer database, or even a family tree greeting card. Others might want to prepare a family fact board game, a fictionalized account of how families merged, or a dramatization of key events in a family's history.

One enrichment cluster facilitator in Arizona engaged in a project with his students that involved walking to a nearby nursing home and partnering each student with a resident. Each student interviewed his or her resident about key events in the resident's life and took notes. Back at the school, they used the computer program Timeliner (https://www.tomsnyder.com/timelinerxe) to create timelines of their residents' lives. They even contacted some of the residents' children and obtained pictures of the residents when they were younger. On the final day, the students presented the timelines to the residents and hung them on the walls inside the nursing home.

By encouraging multiple modes of expression, you allow students to capitalize on their creativity and individual strengths. One of the ways in which enrichment clusters strive to accommodate student differences is to suggest various modes of expression. (Handout 3.1c: Product Planning Guide lists five categories of instructional products and many expression style options.)

Key question 6 focuses on an important part of the facilitator's work. In the real world, almost all work is intended to have an impact on one or more targeted audiences, and in order to find those audiences, you will be serving as a referral agent, promoter, or marketing manager of student work. Within school, student and parent audiences are obvious options and good places to practice and perfect performances and presentations, but young people will begin to view themselves in a much more professional role when you help them seek audiences outside the school. Local newspapers, shopping guides, and city or state magazines are excellent places to submit written work. Public buildings and business offices are often receptive to requests to display the young people's work. Local or state organizations such as historical societies, writer's clubs, civic groups, environmental preservation associations, and advocacy groups also provide opportunities for young investigators, inventors, and entrepreneurs to present their work. You can help young dramatists and filmmakers take their work "on the road" by contacting retirement homes, daycare centers, church groups, or professional organizations.

One group of students who wrote and produced a legal thriller presented a synopsis of the plot at a county bar association meeting.

Your role in helping young people find outlets and audiences in their community should be both advisory and preparatory. You might, for example, suggest that students contact local banks for possible displays, and you also might provide students with the names of bank managers. But after rehearsing their pitch with you and others in their group, the students themselves should make the contacts (using e-mail, telephone, or old-fashioned letter writing), set up the interviews, and be prepared to answer questions that the bank managers might raise. After hearing one student pitch, a shopping mall manager exclaimed, "It's hard to turn down such an enthusiastic group of kids!"

Other opportunities for outlets and audiences outside school abound. Many professional organizations at both state and national levels have newsletters, Twitter, Facebook, Instagram, websites, and blogs, and there are a number of magazines and journals that publish the work of young people. Founded in 1987, *The Concord Review* (http://www.tcr.org) publishes exemplary history essays by secondary students in the English-speaking world. *Time for Kids* (http://www.timeforkids.com/news) is a free news and writing service for young people around the globe. And the print magazines *Creative Kids* (http://www.ckmagazine.org) and *Stone Soup* (http://www.stonesoup.com) consist entirely of stories, poetry, and artwork by young writers and artists. Visiting their websites, you can find information about other publications that take student writing, as well as several free Internet opportunities for young people to share their work.

Almost every topic and area of study has directories that list publishing opportunities for young people. The Directory of Poetry Publishers (Fulton, 2002) includes 21 categories of information on more than 1,900 book and magazine publishers of poetry. *The Writer* (http://www.writermag.com) is another source of information for writing and publishing opportunities, and includes specialty areas such as children's literature, technical writing, and writing for teenage audiences.

All fields of organized knowledge have similar resources. Enter almost any subject area into a search engine and follow the links. Entering "archaeology," for example, led us to numerous resources ranging from newsletters to specialty areas (e.g., underwater archaeology), from places where students can take virtual field trips to active sites where real-time excavations are being conducted. In no time at all, you will find all types of information and resources that deal with the key questions. You will also multiply the options that your students might pursue as your enrichment cluster gets underway.

Contests and competitions are also great outlets and audiences. Most teachers are familiar with science fairs, National History Day, and Math League, but there are thousands of competitions in areas such as photography, fashion design, inventions, greeting cards, play writing, technology, and web design. Preparing for and entering competitions creates a tremendous amount of excitement and enthusiasm in young people, although you should be cautious about using competitions to put pressure on students. Making them aware of competitive opportunities is part of a good coach's job, but the decision to enter a competition should be made by the students themselves. They can find out about suitable competitions by consulting *The Best Competitions for Talented Kids* (Karnes, 2014).

Remember, your job is not to know all of the possible outlets for students' products or the vehicles for reaching different audiences. Simply knowing that resources exist to help find them, having a sample or two to illustrate what typical resources look like, and being able to provide guidance about where and how to search for them encourages young practicing professionals. The very search for outlets and audiences, writing query letters and submitting work for possible publication, presentation, or display, and receiving replies (even negative ones) are all part of the creative process and a major source of motivation for aspiring writers, scientists, artists, and other action-oriented young people.

4. Write your enrichment cluster description. Writing the enrichment cluster description presents special challenges. The description must convey the essence of what this experience is all about in a way that captivates students without being too specific. This task can be especially difficult because of habits formed from too much didactic teaching and established student perceptions of school. The challenge is further complicated because you can't (and shouldn't) specify in the description exactly what students will be doing in the cluster, although you do want to provide some ideas as to the various roles students might take on. Appendix B: Sample Enrichment Cluster Descriptions includes descriptions of several clusters from schools involved in our research to serve as examples for you.

Several suggestions for writing cluster descriptions have emerged from our research. First, at all costs, you must avoid using the word *learn* in the cluster description. Students have come to associate learning in school with the school's traditional information transmission function. Enrichment clusters are different, and you should employ verbs that convey action (doing tasks) rather than transferring and assimilating information (see Figure 4.2). Think about the specific tasks associated with a particular topic or area of study (e.g., in a cluster involving building and marketing compost bins, you might use verbs such as *hammer*, *drill*, *plane*, *weld*, *solder*, *market*, *contact*, *display*, and *sell*).

You should also avoid the words *class* and *club*. Rather than writing, "In this class we will . . . ," use a word that represents the ways in which professionals identify themselves in the adult world. For example, the description of a cluster designed to attract young people with an interest in mapmaking might say, "In the Creative Cartographers Guild, we will design special-purpose maps of places in our town that may be of interest to you (historical, recreational, birdwatching, or others that you will identify)." The word *club* is problematic for political reasons: The general

Action Verbs				
Build	Stack	Balance	Elevate	Sketch
Erect	Transform	Construct	Manufacture	Draft
Make	Create	Assemble	Form	Model
Shape	Design	Visualize	Draw	Originate
Compose	Pattern	Arrange	Organize	Correspond
Dispose	Write	Compile	Mark	Edit
Describe	Engrave	Carve	Record	Outline
Paint	Cover	Spread	Photograph	Lay out
Display	Present	Demonstrate	Illustrate	Diagram
Choreograph	Dance	Cook	Sing	Play
Perform	Act Out	Move	Listen	Direct
Measure	Gauge	Calculate	Compute	Evaluate
Determine	Count	Assess	Quantify	Weigh
Plan	Generate	Start	Imagine	Implement
Divine	Produce	Develop	Apply	Exercise
Nurture	Oversee	Engage	Encourage	Interview
Persuade	Bargain	Suggest	Communicate	Discuss
Synthesize	Experiment	Strategize	Practice	Analyze
Predict	Categorize	Estimate	Teach	Observe
Critique	Review	Examine	Acquire	Support
Defend	Incorporate	Immerse	Embellish	Derive
Elaborate	Explore	Gather	Condense	Problem-solve
Expand	Compare	Contrast	Verify	Problem-find

FIGURE 4.2. Possible action verbs to use in enrichment cluster descriptions.

public typically considers clubs a secondary, less-than-rigorous responsibility of schools. You can, of course, always refer to your cluster as "this enrichment cluster."

Another way to write cluster descriptions is to pose questions about potential student interests and possible types of involvement, such as the following:

- "Do you like to express your feelings by writing poetry or short stories?"
- "Are you concerned about finding better ways to protect wildlife?"
- "Would you like to try your hand at designing fashions for teens?"
- "Have you ever thought about entering a model airplane contest?"
- "Would you like to create your own comic book superhero?"
- "Have you ever considered starting a small business on the Internet?"
- "Could our school produce its own weekly television show?"

Each of these questions relates to a topic around which a cluster might be developed, and yet the questions are open-ended enough to enable a broad range of activities in specific interest areas.

Mentioning opportunities or possibilities for exploration (while avoiding language that implies too much planning and direction on your part) can also grab a student's attention. For example, the description of a cluster on landscaping and interior design might read, "In this cluster, we may explore several different approaches to making our school building and grounds more attractive, or you might design a plan for your own house or garden." The description should convey a sense of opportunity for decision making on the parts of students, and whenever possible, you may want to allude to opportunities for various interests and expression styles within the topic area. The following description announced an enrichment cluster on local history:

> How History Shaped Our Town: People, Events, and Roots
> What was our town like in the 1800s? To do research on this topic, we need historians, techies, mapmakers, photographers, artists, interviewers, and persons who might want to write a script to dramatize one of our town's historical events.

As you begin writing your descriptions, remember: Convey the essence of the experience, captivate students' attention, specify possible roles, use action verbs, avoid defining tasks, and avoid the word *learn*. Keep it exciting and enticing.

After you have written your description, brainstorm a few appealing names for the cluster. Once again, define your group in a real-world (nonschool) way and don't use the words *class* or *club*. Calling an enrichment cluster a guild, society, institute, or task force, or developing a business name, will let students know that enrichment clusters are going to be different from school-as-usual. Try the description and sample titles out on a few of your colleagues or some of your students. Ask if the cluster names and description would make someone want to sign up for the cluster, and don't be afraid to revise based on their feedback. Experiencing this creative planning process is good training for both internalizing inductive learning and launching the cluster.

5. Launch your enrichment cluster. On a practical note, since students will be coming from different classrooms and grade levels, the first thing you will want to do is learn their names, help them to learn one another's names, and make them feel at ease. You can distribute name tags (the ones on neck strings are best) and ask students to wear them at the meetings. It is a good idea to collect the name tags at the end of each session so that they will be available for subsequent sessions. You can do an introductory activity in which students develop a logo for the cluster that they will place on their name tags. Have the students divide into groups to brainstorm ideas, vote to select one, and ask for a volunteer to draw a logo based on the most popular idea. You can then make copies of the logo and let students paste it on their name tags.

Because students who have signed up for your cluster have expressed an interest in the topic, beginning a cluster is usually easier than introducing a new topic in the general classroom. However, it may take some time for students to understand the different approach to learning. A display of some of the products or tools typically used by professionals in your topic area is always a good way to begin. In a cluster on archaeology entitled The Trash Heaps of Mankind, the facilitator showed slides of some famous and local archaeological discoveries (obtained from the state archaeologist). She then organized a short guessing game about what was in a "Mystery Box" in the front of the room. The teacher opened the box to reveal a trowel, a sieve, a pair of gloves, a dust brush, pegs and string, a marking pen, and a camera. She pointed out that these were the main tools of the archaeologist and that an examination of material found in garbage dumps was one of the ways that archaeologists analyze both past and present cultures. A short video of a dig in their own state further built up interest in the work of practicing archaeologists. At a subsequent session, an archaeology professor from a nearby university made a presentation that provided several ideas for local research opportunities and cautioned students about the ethical responsibilities of maintaining site integrity.

A cluster on journalism illustrates additional strategies for exposing students to all the possibilities the cluster offers:

> Let's Go To Press
>
> Have you ever thought about writing for a newspaper or creating your own current events blog? In this cluster, you will have a chance to try out your writing skills on topics that are of special interest to you. Or you might want to explore news photography, desktop publishing, cartooning, interviewing, various blogging platforms, or the business aspects of newspaper publishing. We will visit our local newspaper office and talk with writers, editors, and other persons that produce *The Gazette*.

Sometimes it is easier to introduce students to what people do in particular jobs by beginning with the products they develop and the audiences they intend to impact. You might begin a cluster on journalism by simply asking, "What are all the different types of writing and other kinds of work that you can find in newspaper, magazine, or online publishing?"

On chart paper, the whiteboard, or the smartboard, you can record student responses using a webbing technique such as the one displayed on the left side of Figure 4.3. Proceed to the Outlet/Audience side of the web by asking, "In addition

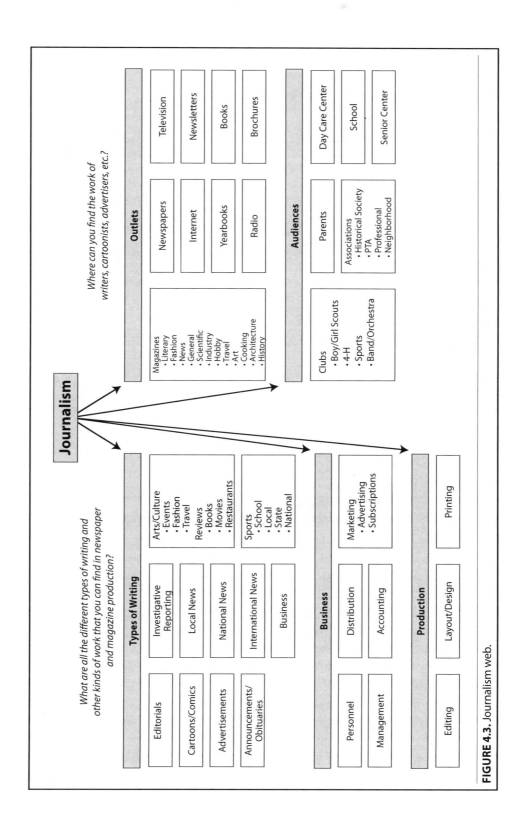

FIGURE 4.3. Journalism web.

to newspapers and magazines, are there other places where we can find the work of writers, cartoonists, advertisers, etc.?"

As a related activity, you might also ask students to find as many different sections of a newspaper as they can to place on a bulletin board. Divide students into groups, provide each group with a set of newspapers, magazines, and scissors, and see which group can generate the most items and the largest variety of items for its section of the bulletin board.

You can also ask students to see if they are interested in working in one or more of the areas depicted on the web diagram. Depending on the size of the group, this approach will enable you to create subgroups that respect student interests. Ask if there are one or more particular modes of expression on which they would like to concentrate. You can also discuss with students a list of possible products they might develop and prioritize the list based on group consensus. Students will need to decide whether there will be one product (e.g., a school newspaper) or various products (e.g., a school newspaper, a Kid's Corner section in the local newspaper, and a closed-circuit school television news program).

6. Escalate content and process. The next step involves the various jobs in the cluster and the division of labor—which should be determined entirely by students. At this step, you must think about how to escalate the level of challenge and the quality of the students' work, an extremely important part of your job. One of the problems we encountered in our research was a failure of some facilitators to escalate the level of content and methodological processes pursued within a cluster. We observed many exciting, fun-filled activities, and this kind of enjoyment of learning is unquestionably one of the most desirable features of a good cluster. However, critics may say that clusters are nothing more than fun and games, or that students carried out their work with existing skills rather than acquiring more advanced skills. You can guard against these criticisms by examining each cluster with an eye toward what constitutes authentic and rigorous content within the field or fields of study around which the cluster is organized. For example, in the cluster mentioned in Chapter 2: What Is an Enrichment Cluster? on designing and marketing birdhouses and feeders, the facilitator began by helping the students obtain books on ornithology, marketing, and advertising as well as how-to books on birdhouse and feeder construction. By encouraging students to consider options that would make their birdhouses and feeders viable products in a competitive marketplace, the facilitator ensured that students went beyond surface facts and engaged in authentic methodologies.

Similarly, in a journalism cluster, a discussion with the librarian and a quick Google search will reveal dozens of resources on general and specific aspects of journalism. These resources range from how-to advice on writing, editing, and lay-out to complex issues about First Amendment rights and freedom of the press. You should not use these books to teach lessons on the required skills, but rather,

suggest that students review the sections applicable to the role that they will play in producing the newspaper. Let them know that you are available to answer questions, help them look for additional resources, and resolve differences of opinion that may arise within a subgroup or between the various subgroups. There may be occasions when it is necessary to teach and rehearse a particular skill (e.g., how to conduct an interview or use a certain computer program or photographic equipment), and any direct teaching should always be targeted toward students who require the skill to address a problem or task necessary to develop the product, performance, or service. You should avoid being the final word on work produced by students. Allow the editors to provide feedback on writing, but be ready to enter the dialogue when strong differences of opinion emerge. Encourage students to make group decisions about deadlines, production schedules, and various options for layout, the use of graphics, and other issues related to style.

When a parent at one school approached the principal about what she described as her "fun-and-games" view of enrichment clusters, we began thinking about some of the clusters we have observed and how teachers have taken very creative steps to "academicize" their clusters. Academicizing a cluster simply means infusing scholarly material and the know-how of professionals to approximate the ways in which experts in a particular field go about studying a topic. Any topic, from basket weaving to making brownies, can be made more academically rigorous. Basket weaving can involve geometry, the experimental testing of materials, and the comparative study of cultures and creative arts. Brownie making can be a launching pad for experimenting with original recipes, developing and illustrating a hometown cookbook, and starting a small business with manufacturing, advertising, sales, accounting, and marketing divisions.

Let's analyze academicizing by reviewing a case study of an enrichment cluster based on quilting. The teacher used a webbing technique and group discussion to examine all the ways that professional quilters examine this area of study. The first step in organizing a cluster is making it known to the student body. The advertisement for the quilting cluster read:

> The Quilting Bee
> Pictures in fabric, family stories, expressions of beauty, geometric shapes, historical documentation. All these things are quilts! And quilters are experts in studying the history of famous people, families, and important places and events.
> Do you want to know the history of quilts, design your own original quilt, find out how they are made, and find out how they have been used? Come to Mrs. De Wet's quilting bee and try your hand at FABRIC ART!

An important thing to remember is that the facilitator does not need to be an expert in quilting; an interest in the topic and a willingness to find helpful resources is an excellent starting point. The facilitator functions mainly as a "guide on the side" by getting the necessary know-how from a few carefully selected books that can be used by both teacher and students. A quick Internet search for this cluster turned up the following three how-to books:

- *Making History: Quilts & Fabrics From 1890-1970* by Barbara Brackman
- *Centennial Stitches: Oklahoma History in Quilts* by Judy Howard
- *Quilting Revealed 101: Beginners Guide to Quilting* by Manuel Ortiz Braschi (Editor)

These books provided the background to get the cluster started, as well as information leading to student discussions and plans for their own work. They helped fill in some of the academic aspects of quilting displayed in the concept web in Figure 4.4. The facilitator might choose to emphasize any feature of the topic at the introductory meeting of the cluster. For our example, this facilitator brought in some quilts from home and others that she borrowed from friends in the community. The first quilt she showed was one her grandmother made from scraps left over from family clothing. Each piece of fabric has a history and connects closely to a family member or event. A patch showing medals won by a family war hero, another about a historical building in their town, and one showing the family coat of arms were discussed from a historical perspective. The teacher developed a great deal of interest and motivation by arranging to have a members of a local quilting club make a presentation and go over some of the basic skills necessary to get started.

Another type of quilt displayed was a memory quilt made by students in a previous cluster as a birthday gift for the facilitator. She told the story of each patch and invited students to touch and examine the quilts, eliciting a discussion on colors, patterns, and fabrics found in each, as well as their construction. She then drew students' attention to the three previously mentioned books and went over the many aspects of quilting. She gave students ample time to page through the books, comment on what interested them, and begin to jot down ideas about possible products, outlets, and audiences for their work. She spent time brainstorming possible topics for historical investigations with the students, and together they developed the following concept web that became a bulletin board display (see Figure 4.4).

Once this web was created, the facilitator surveyed students to see which aspect of quilting interested them. Some students were more interested in the historical aspects of quilting rather than the needlework, but participated enthusiastically by researching the historical background for particular segments of the quilts that were under construction. The teacher discovered that one student was particularly

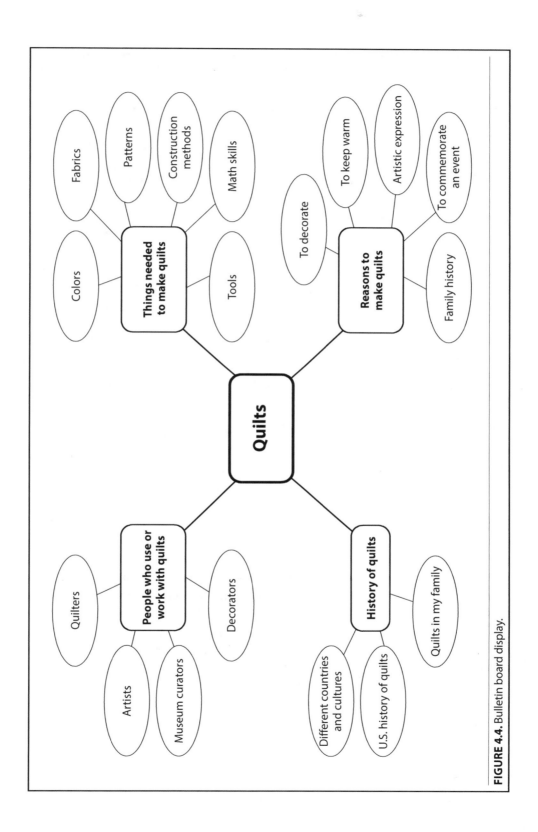

FIGURE 4.4. Bulletin board display.

interested in her own family history and decided to express this history through an original quilt. Several other students were interested in the scientific preservation of quilts and old fabric. This led the teacher to contact a museum employee, who led them to find another person knowledgeable in the preservation of fabrics. One thing about enrichment clusters is that the teacher-as-facilitator follows interest-based leads. This guide-on-the-side role is very different from the traditional teacher role as a disseminator of information.

The teacher asked students to gather in small interest groups and come up with a list of ideas and resources for quilts, and to discuss the research they would need to do in order to make their quilts "tell a story." The teacher also built into the cluster planning and organizational skills by asking each group or individual to complete a Type III Enrichment Management Plan. This plan helped students to focus goals and explore products, outlets, and audiences for their quilting activities. Using a Type III management plan helps students and their facilitators specify the content, resources, methods, and steps they need to take to successfully develop their products and services, including planning for sharing with authentic audiences. The management plan helps to break down what might at the onset seem like an overwhelming project into doable steps, by dividing it into parts and sequencing the steps to completing each part. One group wanted to make baby quilts to donate to a local homeless shelter, and another decided to do a history of their town. The teacher arranged to have a group of ladies from a neighborhood quilting bee teach students some basic skills necessary to get started on their own work.

The teacher also helped to guide students in planning their activities, finding the necessary resources, and gaining the skills needed to complete their projects. The student interested in her family history needed to learn oral history data-gathering skills to record interviews with family members. Another how-to book on this skill was ordered by the school librarian and resulted in a whole new set of academic research skills, illustrating that quilting, far from being a fun-and-games subject, is a topic that can involve many historical, artistic, and sociological research skills. The students interested in family history decided to publish a small book complete with family trees and family photographs. Members from the visiting quilting bee agreed to serve as mentors and helped these young quilter historians in the construction of their projects. An exhibition of the students' quilts was arranged at a local fabric store, and some of the quilts were displayed in public buildings before being donated to a local homeless shelter.

WHY IS ACADEMICIZING ENRICHMENT CLUSTERS IMPORTANT?

In this day and age of relentless pressure to raise achievement test scores, we have witnessed a growing lack of genuine student engagement in learning and an epidemic of boredom. Although our research has shown that the kinds of learning experiences that define enrichment clusters make learning engaging and enjoyable, and that these experiences do, in fact, result in improved achievement, many education leaders have opted for highly prescriptive drill-and-practice approaches to test score improvement. More than a few administrators have told us that they would like to initiate a cluster program, but test preparation in its most repetitive form must take precedence.

For this reason it falls to us to be sure we can show specific examples of academic content and thinking skills in our enrichment clusters. The work that the students in the quilting cluster did in historical research, interviewing, geometric design, fabric preservation, and the oral and visual presentation used in sharing their work need to be highlighted in any reports, press releases, and presentations made about the cluster, and parents should be provided with a checklist of all the important academic skills implicit in the work. Fun and engagement are, unquestionably, important goals, but we can't leave ourselves open to criticism because of the external pressures being placed on schools as a result of test score mania.

Another thing we have learned from teachers who have worked hard to academicize their clusters is that they have shown pride in the new content area knowledge and research skills they themselves have gained about topics of interest. Many teachers have said that they are applying some of the strategies used in enrichment clusters to their regular classroom teaching, and in so doing, they have observed increases in student engagement and motivation.

ENSURING AUTHENTICITY IN ENRICHMENT CLUSTERS: GATHERING ORIGINAL DATA

Over many years of working with students in high-end learning situations, we have discovered that there is a certain magic associated with gathering original data. Young people are surrounded with an almost infinite number of data-gathering opportunities, and these opportunities provide them with the possibility of creating new knowledge. This knowledge may not be new for all mankind, but it may be original in a local and relative way. So, for example, when a group of elementary students spent an entire school year gathering and analyzing samples of rainwater for sulfur and nitrogen oxide emissions, the main pollutants responsible for acid rain, they were able to prepare a scientifically respectable report about the extent of acid rain that was falling in their region of the country. Their teacher helped them obtain a standard rain gauge and a kit for testing acidity, items that can be found in almost any science equipment catalog. Additional resources enabled these students to prepare statistical and graphic summaries of their data, compare their findings with data from national and regional reports (easily accessible online), and design maps showing acid rain trends over time and across geographic regions. The data provided the excitement and motivation to study environmental and health problems associated with various types of pollution, and they found receptive audiences for their work among state environmental protection groups, the U. S. Environmental Protection Agency, and the National Weather Bureau. The students also exchanged their report and findings with a group doing a similar study at a school in England, which they located by entering "acid rain" into an Internet search engine.

Original contributions to almost every field of knowledge are based on data gathered through the use of one or more instruments. Even artists use cameras, audio and video recorders, sketch pads, or clippings from magazines to record sights, sounds, colors, and impressions that might form the basis for an original painting, composition, set design, or costume. We have included a partial listing of instruments students might use in Figure 4.5. Some instruments are complex and may require special training; others are as basic as a pencil and a tally sheet. One group of students investigating gender equity simply tallied the number of male versus female protagonists for all books in the fiction section of their school library. One of their products included a recommended list of books featuring female protagonists, and another was a petition for the purchase of books from their list. Another group of students used tally sheets, plastic cups, a scale, and a measuring beaker as part of their investigation into lunchroom waste and dietary preferences among their schoolmates. This study also included a follow-up questionnaire, the results of which were analyzed by grade and gender, and the group made recommendations to the school district dietician for meals that were more in line with student preferences.

Most data in the social sciences are gathered through surveys, rating scales, and interviews. Several excellent books help young people develop these types of instruments, and some of these how-to books also contain guidelines for various ways to tabulate and analyze the data (see Appendix C: Methodological Resources). Instrument development is an important part of the scientific process and provides opportunities to guide students through very professional methods such as brainstorming, refining and focusing survey items, field testing draft versions of the instrument, writing good directions, data gathering, tabulation, analysis, and reporting.

Interview	Water Test Kit	Sextant
Questionnaire	Oxygen Analyzer	Thermometer
Rating Scale	Colorimeter	Anemometer
Rank Order Instrument	Air Flow Indicator	Hydrometer
Observation Record	Magnifier	Barometer
Sociometric Device	Microscope	Audiometer
Q Sort	Telescope	Eye Chart
Test	Litmus Paper/pH Meter	Blood Pressure Monitor
Salt Analyzer	Scale	Color Blindness Test
Conductivity Meter	Ruler	Pedometer
Metal Detector	Tape Measure	Physiograph
Dissecting Kit	Volt Meter	Maze
Microtome	Amp Meter	Camera
Radiation Detector	Ohm Meter	Voice Recorder
Solar Cell	Light Meter	Video Recorder
Micrometer	Sound Meter	Excavation Tool
Biofeedback Monitor	Spectroscope	GPS (iPhone / iPad)
Respiratory Flow Meter	Oscilloscope	http://www.polleverywhere.com

FIGURE 4.5. Data-gathering instruments students can use.

Once students have gathered original data, there are numerous ways in which they can professionalize their work. They can use standard research techniques such as making comparisons between various groups (age, grade, gender, activities, preferences) and across time periods. Depending on the age and math skills of students, data analyses can range from simple pie charts to much more sophisticated methods. Statistical computer programs and visual display software can help escalate the quality of student products.

One of the best ways to help students develop a data-gathering frame of reference is to familiarize them with the kinds of instruments professionals use in their respective fields of inquiry. Looking through how-to books or consulting professionals are good ways of learning about instruments and their use in particular fields. There are also several good books about conducting research in various domains that provide both teachers and students with ideas about data gathering and making the best use of data in comparative ways. Three of our favorites are *Chi Square Pie Charts and Me* (Baum, Gable, & List, 1987), *Looking for Data in All The Right Places* (Starko & Schack, 1992), and *Research Comes Alive!* (Schack & Starko, 1998; see Appendix C: Methodological Resources for complete descriptions).

Although instrument selection and data gathering would normally flow from the research questions that students want to investigate, there may be occasions when familiarizing students with instruments used within their own general area of interest will help generate ideas for a study. For example, a group of students interested in physiology learned how to use instruments that record blood pressure, body temperature, and expository flow (the amount of air you can blow from your lungs in one breath). They brainstormed various studies they might conduct using their new skills and decided to examine before and after differences (pre and post, to use research jargon) in these physiological measures with an experimental group that carried out a specified set of exercises and a control group that did not exercise. The students introduced several variations on the exercise routines based on research about different muscle groups to create a thoughtful series of coordinated studies.

A little data goes a long way in helping students feel like real researchers and do the advanced work that escalates the level of content and methodology to produce high-quality products. If you compare this kind of experience with the traditional approach to student research—looking up information—you immediately see the value of helping students develop a data-gathering frame of reference.

PUTTING IT ALL TOGETHER

The possibilities are truly endless when one moves into the role of facilitator and encourager. Students gain knowledge and skills, but do so in the context of meaningful, self-driven courses of action. A final example illustrates how all the steps come together to create a world-class enrichment cluster in which a facilitator and students work together to explore a topic and offer something unique to the school and community.

> Planet Green
> Are you interested in the environment, and are you an explorer and problem solver at heart? In this cluster, you will have the opportunity to explore, gather data, and take direct action about environmental issues that concern you.

A classroom teacher developed Planet Green for interested elementary school students who had a passion for environmental issues. The facilitator was interested in the environment, but she had never taught it as a subject and initially wondered if she had the expertise to facilitate such a cluster. After discussing the idea with program leaders who helped her identify resources and potential community experts, she decided to go ahead and learn with the students. On the first day of the cluster, she inventoried the 20 student participants about their specific environmental

interests and developed a list of a wide variety of topics. She then asked the group to discuss the topics and narrow the list to the three issues that they were most interested in tackling during the cluster. These three issues focused on the quality of local water, a possible new landfill in their county, and local endangered species. From this list two groups formed: one that wanted to work toward stopping the landfill and another that wanted to raise local awareness about endangered species in the region. Together, the facilitator and students began to gather resources about the problems that the students had chosen as their focus. She invited the county commissioner to discuss zoning and political action with the landfill group. The students suggested bringing in a refuse expert from the local university, and they began an Internet search to identify other resources that would help them understand and act on the landfill situation. The facilitator helped the students locate an expert and make contact with the media. Some students worked with the local television studio, and others worked with a local reporter as they identified issues associated with the landfill. By reviewing the permits, the facilitator and students discovered that although their community only accounted for five tons of garbage per week, the landfill owners had made deals to bring in as many as 60 tons of garbage each week from communities in states thousands of miles away. Armed with this information, they began to organize strategies for community mobilization and political action. As a result of their work, the landfill was unable to gain approval to operate.

The other group, which was studying endangered species, was able to assist the landfill group when they discovered that the wetland neighboring the proposed site was home to an endangered species of turtle. This group invited local biologists to help them understand the regional flora and fauna. They were amazed by the biodiversity of their own community and hypothesized that few people were aware of the different types of plants and animals that existed "right here at home." To test their hypothesis, they created and administered a community survey and tallied the results. They found that there was little public awareness of the 10 animal and 15 plant species in their region that were endangered. Working with a local biologist and botanist, they developed a pamphlet that described the endangered species and listed action steps that would help protect these species. They used the landfill group's connection with the local news and were featured on a special weekend broadcast. As a result of the publicity, local businesses decided to distribute the pamphlets. They developed a public service informational broadcast featured on local news that informed community members of three endangered animal and 12 endangered plant species and ways people could protect them.

At the conclusion of the cluster, the facilitator commented that she had learned as much as the students. Her role had been mostly to assist the students with locating experts and resources and help them plan and carry out their actions. She also reflected on her role of modeling for students how to gain expertise and knowledge concerning an area of interest. She was convinced that she had shown students how to learn, and that being an expert was something attainable and not a requisite to beginning a productive investigation.

We would like to close this chapter by sharing two inspirational exemplars from our advanced Confratute strand.

Hair for Hope

Hair for Hope was a service-related cluster that grew out of interest from a group of upper elementary girls who knew they wanted to help people with cancer. Through their research, students found out that many women lose their hair due to cancer treatments. They also found out about several organizations that donate wigs to women with cancer. The girls interviewed two oncologists in Athens, GA, and were even able to visit one of the doctor's offices to see what patients experience and get ideas about how they could help people with cancer. Through their collection of interview, observation, and research data, the students ultimately decided to organize an event called Hair for Hope. They discovered a corporate-sponsored service project through the company Pantene Pro V called "Beautiful Lengths." With this project, people were able to donate hair for wigs to be made for cancer patients. The students sent out letters to encourage other students and teachers to donate eight inches of their hair for Pantene Pro V Beautiful Lengths. They contacted local hair stylists, make-up artists, and nail artists to volunteer their services for the event. In the end, more than 20 students and teachers donated hair to Hair for Hope. These donors gathered to have their locks trimmed and received hair, make-up, and nail services in return. The girls in the group also created a Renzulli Learning Assignment about cancer that the participants could explore while they were waiting to get their hair cut, make-up done, and nails painted.

Scientist Exploration

The students came up with a list of scientific areas they would like to research and decided to focus on five. Each week the students focused on a new area and conducted experiments or activities that scientists in these fields might conduct. After the 5 weeks, the students created brochures to inform other people about these fields. Some additional extension ideas were allowing the students to create scientist trading cards, how-to videos for science experiments, or living museums for an important scientist in that field. The students came up with the list of ideas and decided where they wanted to start. In addition, they researched scientists in that field for their products. (If able, students could spend some time researching actual experiments that could be done during the following weeks to match up with the chosen scientific field.) Brochures or trading cards could be passed out at a school fair. In addition, the student could also conduct experiments for other classes, or assist in helping other students to conduct these experiments.

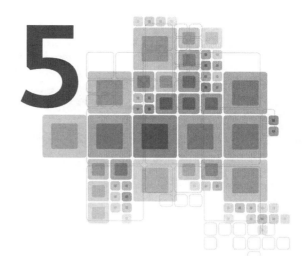

5

STAFF DEVELOPMENT AND PROGRAM EVALUATION

The center for teacher education is not the university: It is the school in which the teacher works.

—Elliot Eisner

Appropriate staff development and support can be the difference between success and failure. The staff development aspect of implementing an enrichment cluster program can be both formal and informal and should respond to the needs of those involved. This chapter offers specific suggestions and activities in the following six categories: 1) Developing Capacity; 2) Enhancing Understanding, Knowledge, and Background; 3) Putting Information Into Context; 4) Putting Knowledge to Work; 5) Creating Ongoing Support; and 6) Using Evaluation Data to Improve the Program.

For each category, we describe a variety of professional development activities that have been successful in our work with program implementation during the past 20 years. Program participants need not do all the activities, and we encourage those in charge of staff development to choose and adapt the activities and methods best suited to their populations. However, some activities are essential (as noted in their descriptions) and must be done before beginning the program.

We believe that staff development is cyclical and ongoing. It is impossible to teach everyone everything that they need to know about enrichment clusters prior to implementation. In the beginning, the goal of staff development is to engender the attitudes, understanding, and confidence that will allow people to move forward with implementation. Initial activities should also create a feeling of ownership and involvement in the program, the processes, and the always-present need for refinement. Ownership, involvement, and a "we-can-make-it-better" attitude will ultimately create a world-class program of high-end learning for all students that is a solid part of the culture of the school.

As with any new program, it helps to acknowledge at the outset that there will be challenges and glitches. Program leaders need to emphasize to all participants that criticism is welcome. However, criticism should always be accompanied by suggestions for possible solutions. This simple ground rule forces staff to move beyond general complaining to brainstorming and attaining solutions. By agreeing to be solution-focused toward problems, staff begin the process poised for success and for a continuously improving program based on feedback, changes, and buy-in.

CATEGORY 1:
DEVELOPING CAPACITY

Why are enrichment clusters important? Will students benefit? How can we afford the time and the specialized materials needed? Do I have the skills? How much more work will these clusters cause me? Any new program raises a flurry of questions. The activities outlined in this section help school personnel examine these questions and others, such as *Why do we educate children?*, *What do we and our students actually remember from school?*, and *Why did we become teachers?* Such discussions set the stage for program buy-in and development. In addition, these activities help colleagues get to know one another and create a better sense of community within the school.

Program leaders should conduct Activity 1.1: Is Anybody Listening? as a bare minimum, and may repeat it at various times throughout staff development to ensure that teachers feel that their input matters and that their questions are being answered. Activity 1.2: Skills We Bring With Us and Activity 1.3: What Do We Want for Students? are recommended, not required, but we believe them to be valuable tools for introducing teachers to the concept of student-driven learning and to the purposes of enrichment clusters. Activity 1.4: What Do I Remember? is an alternative to Activity 1.3 that can be conducted with any facilitators who are not teachers.

ACTIVITY 1.1

ACTIVITY 1.1
IS ANYBODY LISTENING?

Time: 10–15 minutes

Setting: Participants at tables

Materials: Markers, chart paper (or smartphone and a call-in data site)

Designation: Required

Begin by asking groups or individuals to generate a list of questions, issues, and concerns they might have about the enrichment cluster program. Then ask each group to share its top questions, concerns, and issues with the whole group, instructing participants to listen carefully and avoid repeating issues that have already been raised. Move around the room, and as all issues, concerns, and questions are shared, record them for later reference on chart paper with markers. Use the list as points of departure for discussion. This activity helps with teacher buy-in and ensures that participants' questions are thoroughly addressed.

SKILLS WE BRING WITH US

Time: 35–40 minutes

Setting: Participants in groups at tables

Materials: Handout 1.2a: Have You Ever Been Involved?, Handout 1.2b: Who? What? How?, chart paper, markers

Designation: Recommended

Because many teachers are apprehensive when it comes to new initiatives, this activity should be carried out early in the planning process. Furthermore, teachers have been barraged in recent years by so many "new things" that require major changes in their teaching repertoire that initiatives are often greeted with a "here we go again" attitude. This activity helps teachers analyze the kinds of work they have done in nontraditional learning situations and lets them reach the conclusion that they already have the skills necessary for facilitating an unstructured learning environment such as an enrichment cluster.

Begin the activity by giving everyone a copy of Handout 1.2a: Have You Ever Been Involved?. Ask participants to divide into groups based on the three main categories listed on the handout (sports; clubs/extracurricular activities; and written, visual, and performing arts). If one group is particularly large, they can further divide into subgroups within each of the three areas. Distribute Handout 1.2b: Who? What? How?.

Provide each group with a piece of chart paper and ask that they number and label the chart with the four areas for discussion listed on Handout 1.2b: Who? What? How? (Students, Structure, Student Role, and Facilitator Role). Suggest that they leave enough space between items to record comments, and allow groups approximately 20 minutes to answer the questions based on the collective experiences of those in the group. Focusing on one point at a time, allow each group to report to the larger group. Call attention to commonalities between each group's responses. The following commonalities came to light in our research.

1. Students
 - Interested in the topic or activity; almost always attended voluntarily
 - Usually varied in age
 - Able to contribute different skills (i.e., not everyone in the club, team, or group had to do the same tasks; some could write, some could direct, some could paint sets, etc.)

2. Structure
- More informal than regular classrooms
- More movement as opposed to sitting and listening
- Time varied according to the task
- Special equipment, facilities, and resources sometimes needed

3. Student Role
- More direct, hands-on involvement
- Divisions of labor—not everyone doing the same thing
- Had to develop a product or prepare for a performance
- Concerned about meeting deadlines
- Depended on working cooperatively with others
- Motivated to practice, improve, and perfect what they were doing
- Was helpful to others

4. Facilitator Role
- Less direct teaching
- More of a guide on the side than instructor
- More responsibility given to students

HAVE YOU EVER BEEN INVOLVED?

Have you ever been involved as a coach, advisor, facilitator, leader, or guide in any of the following groups or activities?

SPORTS

Soccer	Baseball
Football	Softball
Field Hockey	Swimming
Gymnastics	Diving
Basketball	Track and Field

CLUBS/EXTRACURRICULAR ACTIVITIES

Future Problem Solving	Boy Scouts
4-H	Girl Scouts
National History Day	Model UN
Junior Achievement	Photography Club
Cooking Club	Outward Bound
Invention Convention	Future Farmers of America
Mock Trial	Service Clubs

WRITTEN, VISUAL, AND PERFORMING ARTS

Drama Productions	Yearbook
Newspaper	Computer/Graphic Design
Band	Fashion Design
Creative Writing Workshop	Video/Filmmaking
Chorus	

HANDOUT 1.2B
WHO? WHAT? HOW?

Based on your experience in a club, sports team, performing arts group, or other group formed around a specific topic or activity, answer the following questions.

1. Students
    - Discuss who was in the group.

2. Structure
    - Discuss organizational and physical aspects of the group—time (hours/minutes), duration (weeks/months), location, special equipment needed, etc.

3. Student Role
    - What did members of the group do?
    - How did members of the group do it?
    - Why did members of the group do it?

4. Facilitator Role
    - What did you do?
    - What different roles did you play?

ACTIVITY 1.3
WHAT DO WE WANT FOR STUDENTS?

Time: 15–20 minutes

Setting: Participants at tables

Materials: School mission statement, markers, chart paper

Designation: Recommended

The goal of this activity is to help participants recenter themselves in the context of a high-pressure educational system that has lost sight of some of what is truly important in education. Have small groups of participants generate what they hope students will gain after 13 years of education (K–12). List these ideas on chart paper. Ask participants what happens in school to facilitate these hopes. (We have found that only a few items are actually curricular in nature; instead, most center around the big issues of life: productivity, happiness, creativity, citizenship, and personal and social development.)

Pass out copies of the school's mission statement (which is usually full of "good stuff" about maximizing individual potentials, developing productive citizens, developing students who can think and act in a democratic society, and honoring diversity). Discuss the mission statement in the context of the list that participants generated. Point out that enrichment clusters allow teachers to focus on much of what they (and the school) value, thus giving participants a way to connect their and the school's ideals to something they can actually do.

ACTIVITY 1.4
WHAT DO I REMEMBER?

Time: 15–30 minutes

Setting: Participants at tables

Materials: Markers, chart paper

Designation: Optional

An alternative to Activity 1.3, this activity works well with potential facilitators who are not teachers. Begin the activity by dividing participants into small groups to discuss the question "What do you remember about school from when you were a student?" Ask for volunteers from each group to report on the highlights of their discussion, and record responses on chart paper. Responses may vary, but many will center around several areas, including teachers, extracurricular activities, special projects, and students who shared an intense interest. You may also want to pose the follow-up question "What do you want your students to remember?" By asking potential facilitators to examine their own experiences, they then begin to consider what kind of memories schools are building for their students as well as what kind of experiences they ought to deliver. Tie the ensuing discussion to the concept of an enrichment cluster program by emphasizing that the clusters allow adults to work with students in areas of mutual interest toward a meaningful product or service, something that is too infrequent in the context of ordinary school. Emphasize the chance to involve all students in opportunities that will build quality memories.

CATEGORY 2:
ENHANCING UNDERSTANDING, KNOWLEDGE, AND BACKGROUND

When implementing a new enrichment cluster program, everyone needs to have the same information regarding the philosophy, goals, intentions, and expected outcomes. We suggest that each member of the faculty and any volunteer facilitators have access to this book and are involved in basic informational sessions about the program. The following activities introduce potential facilitators to the specifics of an enrichment cluster program and help them examine the difference between enrichment clusters and other forms of teaching such as minicourses and simulations.

EVERYTHING YOU NEED TO KNOW

Time: 20–60 minutes

Setting: Any group setting

Materials: Introductory PowerPoint slideshow available at http://www.gifted.uconn.edu; click on "Enrichment Clusters" link

Designation: Required

The purpose of this activity is to introduce enrichment clusters and present a logical argument for implementing an enrichment cluster program. Begin this staff development session with a brief overview of the following points. Each point includes suggested content you might want to cover.

Why clusters? Emphasize that clusters create a special time for schoolwide enrichment and ensure that all students and staff have opportunities for engaging in enrichment learning and teaching. The focus is interest-based, strength-based high-end learning for all students.

What are clusters? Explain that enrichment clusters are specially designated blocks of time occurring during the regular school day when people with common interests come together to explore a topic. They are student-driven, teacher-facilitated authentic learning experiences in which students apply advanced content and authentic methods to develop products and services for real-world audiences. Who wouldn't be excited to become involved in such a great opportunity—one in which students and adult facilitators work together in their areas of strengths, interests, and passions? In effect, this program extends activities typically used in gifted education to all students.

Why do clusters when there is already so much to do? Discuss the goal of involving all teachers and students in areas of strength and interest to develop real products and services using authentic methods. Revisit how this goal fits with the mission of educating children. Suggest that skills learned in facilitating clusters can transfer back to the classroom, thus strengthening the general education program.

Emphasize the fact that not all students have had opportunities to become involved in this type of learning in a typical school day. This situation is especially true for some at-risk students who are at the center of discipline problems. Ask whether enrichment cluster opportunities might help engage these students by creating a place where their strengths and interests are valued and used.

Have the group consider the question "How can we afford not to take the time to do something as important as developing an enrichment cluster program for students and staff?" Emphasize staff talent development—having the opportunity to work with students who share an interest with a facilitator to create "great things."

Revisit the mission statement to see if participants agree that all children ought to have some time in school to work in areas of strength and interest together with others who have similar interests.

THE GOOD, THE BAD, AND THE . . .

Time: 45–60 minutes

Setting: Any group setting

Materials: Handout 2.2a: Sample Descriptions, Handout 2.2b: Evaluating Clusters

Designation: Required

Before beginning this activity, make sure all participants have been introduced to enrichment clusters in Activity 2.1: Everything You Need to Know. Distribute copies of Handout 2.2a: Sample Descriptions and Handout 2.2b: Evaluating Clusters, and ask them to evaluate the merit of each cluster. Included in the sample descriptions are two or three examples of clusters that could be improved. Notice that the participants will use the elements of great clusters (i.e., student driven; advanced content; authentic methods; real audience, product, or service) to evaluate the quality of these sample clusters. Because the clusters are samples, they provide a nonthreatening way to examine, criticize, and improve someone else's cluster. I always tell participants that everyone can offer a better cluster than the volcano example! Solicit suggestions on how the clusters might be improved. (This discussion leads into Activity 3.1: Developing an Enrichment Cluster.)

HANDOUT 2.2A
SAMPLE DESCRIPTIONS

SAMPLE CLUSTER A: VOLCANOES

Facilitators instructed their fourth-, fifth-, and sixth-grade students in how to build paper mâché volcanoes and provided them with the necessary materials. Students spent 6 weeks creating their volcanoes, working primarily on construction and painting their finished products. On the last day, parents attended and watched as the students added red food coloring to vinegar that they placed in a cup in the cones of their volcanoes. One by one, students then placed baking soda into the mixture of vinegar and food coloring and "exploded" their volcanoes.

SAMPLE CLUSTER B: TO BE OR NOT . . . POETRY

Students and facilitators decided to study poetic forms and create a publication of original work that they would distribute to classrooms, libraries, coffee shops, and waiting rooms at local doctor's and dentist's offices. They also decided to hold a contest for the best cover design for their publication. Further discussion and brainstorming led to the implementation of a poetry reading night. To set up the poetry reading night, they contacted the Actor's Guild cluster and asked if any members would be interested in performing an interpretive reading of the selections. They also decided to contact the Young Artists' cluster to solicit some expressive artwork for publication and display. The culmination of this cluster was a community poetry reading held at a local business, where copies of the publication were distributed. Both local radio and television media covered the event, which has now become annual.

SAMPLE CLUSTER C: CHOCOLATE, HOW SWEET IT IS

The facilitator, an admitted chocoholic, worked with students to teach them all about where chocolate comes from, how it is made, differences in production and quality, the uses of chocolate, what is known about chocolate scientifically, and the history of chocolate. Students were involved in tasting and making creations using chocolate. For a final product, they organized a chocolate tasting seminar for others in the school and handed out brochures with the essential facts about chocolate that they learned in the cluster.

SAMPLE CLUSTER D: ENVIRONMENTAL STUDIES

This cluster was advertised to interested middle school students who had a passion for environmental issues. On the first day, the facilitator inventoried students concerning their specific environmental interests. She then asked the group to discuss the issues and narrow the list to the three issues in which they were most interested. These three issues turned out to be quality of local water, a possible new landfill in their county, and local endangered species. From this list, two groups formed, one that wanted to work toward stopping the landfill and another that wanted to raise awareness of endangered species in the local region. Their work helped prevent the landfill from gaining approval to operate, and they developed a pamphlet (featured on local news) that informed community members of three endangered animal and 12 endangered plant species, together with a list of action steps for assisting with the conservation of these species.

SAMPLE CLUSTER E: READ ALL ABOUT IT

This cluster was set up as a means for producing the school newspaper. The facilitator brainstormed with students about what features ought to be included in the paper and discussed the aspects of newspaper production. Someone in charge of producing the local paper made a presentation and answered questions. They then began to chart a course, schedule, and list of content for their own production. Students discussed the various roles, divided them up by interest in particular jobs (e.g., photographer, layout, copy editor, reporter, feature writer, marketing, etc.), and got to work on producing a biweekly publication. Their audience was the entire school.

HANDOUT 2.2B
EVALUATING CLUSTERS

Use the following questions to evaluate the sample clusters.

1. How well does this sample cluster address the following elements of a good cluster?
   - Advanced Content
   - Authentic Methods
   - Product and/or Service
   - Student Driven
   - Authentic Audience

2. How could this cluster be improved to more accurately reflect good cluster philosophy and practice?

CATEGORY 3:
PUTTING INFORMATION INTO CONTEXT

When discussing and describing any new program or concept, it is easy to assume a deeper understanding among participants than actually exists. People may nod in agreement, but not fully understand what is necessary or have the skills to proceed effectively. To increase both understanding and efficacy, we suggest using the following simulations. Our experience has shown that Activity 3.1: Developing an Enrichment Cluster can make the difference between implementation of authentic clusters and teacher-directed minicourses.

ACTIVITY 3.1
DEVELOPING AN ENRICHMENT CLUSTER

Time: 45–60 minutes

Setting: Space for groups of 6–10 people to work together

Materials: Previously completed Handout 3.1a: Inspiration Survey, Handout 3.1b: Developing an Enrichment Cluster, Handout 3.1c: Product Planning Guide, Handout 2.2b: Evaluating Clusters

Designation: Required

We believe that this activity is crucial to understanding the nature of and process for creating a great cluster. Participants have consistently indicated that this activity crystallizes the vision and theory and helps them develop authentic clusters rather than minicourses.

Be sure to ask potential facilitators to bring a previously completed copy of Handout 3.1a: Inspiration Survey to this session. Tell participants that this activity will involve everyone in the conceptualization of a cluster, either in the role of facilitator or student. Ask participants to briefly review their responses to Handout 3.1a: Inspiration Survey, and invite volunteers to take on the roles of facilitators for clusters in which they are interested. Ask the volunteers to name their cluster and record the volunteer's name and the cluster name on chart paper. You will need one cluster facilitator for every 6–10 people in the group.

Next, have the cluster facilitators pick up a copy of Handout 3.1b: Developing an Enrichment Cluster, Handout 3.1c: Product Planning Guide, some chart paper, and markers. Ask the rest of the participants to choose one of the clusters. (Some participants may ask whether they are to role play as adults or children; either works well.) Instruct the groups to answer the questions in Handout 3.1b: Developing an Enrichment Cluster and be prepared to report their results to the larger group. Thirty minutes is a sufficient amount of working time, but you might announce when 5 or 10 minutes remain.

Sample responses to each question based on a cluster on creating displays were as follows:

- *What will the name of this cluster be?* Dioramas; Creating Spaces; Models, Inc.; Visual Display Experts.
- *What will the product or service from this cluster be?* Museum exhibits, window displays, design consulting, architectural planning.

- *What roles will cluster members assume?* Designer, researcher, publicity person, developer, construction supervisor, artist.
- *What advanced content, resources, and method will the cluster require?* How to build to scale, historical facts, what types of materials to use, problem finding, critical and creative problem solving, authentic information related to the selected problem or task, marketing strategies, artistic renditions, graphics and visual artist resources.
- *Who will the authentic audience for the product or service be?* A model public transportation system that could be submitted to the town, a dinosaur display to be used in classrooms with younger students, a model of a favorite book to be displayed in the public library, store window displays concerning topics of interest to increase public awareness.

After the groups have developed ideas for their clusters, ask them to share their "mock clusters" using Handout 2.2b: Evaluating Clusters from Activity 2.2 as a basis for discussion. This discussion will help reinforce the nature and philosophy of the clusters. Encourage participants to discuss different directions that the cluster might take with different participants, and emphasize the fact that student interests really should drive the clusters and the activities within them.

HANDOUT 3.1A:
INSPIRATION SURVEY

PART A: TARGETING MY IDEAL TEACHING AND LEARNING SITUATION

The purpose of this survey is to help you examine your interests, experiences, and talents with an eye toward developing an ideal teaching and learning situation. The questionnaire is not a test, and there are no right or wrong answers. Past, present, and future interests and experiences can serve as the basis for a rich, authentic educational experience for both you and your students. In short: If you could share anything with a group of interested students, what would it be?

Read through the questionnaire and give your answers careful consideration. Answer honestly and completely. When you've completed the survey, review your answers with the following question in mind: If I could share one of my interests in a learning situation, what would it be?

PROFESSIONAL EXPERIENCES

1. What is your favorite subject to teach?

    _____

    _____

    _____

2. List any special units you've developed for your classroom.

    _____

    _____

    _____

3. List any areas of knowledge, such as astronomy, photography, geology, geography, archaeology, or any other "ologies" or "ographies" in which you have an interest. Circle your favorite area.

    _____

    _____

    _____

4. Name one thing you have always wanted to teach but never had the opportunity to teach.

_____

_____

_____

5. List any special courses or programs you have taught or would like to teach.

_____

_____

_____

6. Imagine that you have received a federal grant to develop some innovative curricular materials. The only stipulations are that (1) the materials should span two to three grade levels, (2) the materials must focus on activities that are not ordinarily included in regular textbooks or curricular guides, and (3) you must state the general and specific areas and the topical focus of the materials. Fill in the information below on your materials that would meet these stipulations.

Grade levels	**General Curricular Area(s) Specified**
___ Preschool	___ Mathematics
___ Primary (1-3)	___ Science
___ Elementary (4-6)	___ Humanities
___ Junior High (7-9)	___ Social Sciences
___ High School (10-12)	___ Language Arts
___ College	___ Music
___ Special Populations (specify)	___ Drama
_____	___ Art
___ Other _____	___ Other _____

Briefly describe the topical focus of the materials and innovative approaches you would develop.

_____

_____

_____

7. Imagine that you can invite four individuals (living or dead, famous or not) to give a series of lectures (or workshops) in your classroom related to some aspect of your interests or course content. Whom would you invite?

    _____

    _____

    _____

    _____

    From your choices listed above, pick your first choice and briefly explain why you picked this person.

    _____

    _____

    _____

8. Briefly describe the one thing that you feel has been your most creative contribution to teaching.

    _____

    _____

    _____

9. Describe something that you have done to help a single child (or small group of children) develop personally, creatively, or academically, but that did not involve instructing or directly teaching.

    _____

    _____

    _____

PERSONAL EXPERIENCES

10. List the clubs, organizations, and extracurricular activities in which you have been involved during each of the following stages of your life (include hobbies and services):

    Elementary School:

    _____

Secondary School:

_____

College:

_____

Adult:

_____

11. List any work you've published.

_____

12. Where have you traveled?

_____

13. Which place do you consider the most special and why?

_____

14. What do you do in your spare time? If there were no limitations, what would you do in your spare time?

_____

_____

_____

15. Have you ever done anything creative on your own (e.g., written poetry, composed music, organized political action, started an organization or business, etc.)? List some of the things you have done (beginning as far back as you can remember) that were not related to school assignments, extracurricular activities, or activities organized by clubs.

_____

_____

_____

_____

_____

16. What cause would you take up if you had the time?

_____

_____

_____

_____

_____

PART B: DEVELOPING MY IDEAL
TEACHING AND LEARNING SITUATION

After reviewing your responses to Part A of this questionnaire, consider which of your interests you would enjoy sharing with students. Answer the following questions and use your answers as a basis for developing a vision about what might take place in your own ideal teaching and learning situation.

1. If I could share one of my interests in a learning situation, what would it be?

_____

2. What do people with an interest in this area do? List as many different ideas as you can.

_____

_____

_____

_____

_____

3. What materials and resources are needed to address this interest area? Check off those items that you already have. Make notes by those you can obtain.

_____

_____

_____

_____

4. What products or services might be produced or offered by people with an interest in this area? List as many varied ideas as you can. Circle those that you think you could adapt to use with students.

_____

_____

_____

_____

_____

HANDOUT 3.1B:
DEVELOPING AN ENRICHMENT CLUSTER

As a group, answer the following questions for your cluster topic.

1. What will the name of this cluster be?

    _____

2. What will the product(s) or service(s) from this cluster be?

    _____

    _____

    _____

3. What roles will cluster members assume?

    _____

    _____

    _____

4. What advanced content, resources, and methods will the cluster require?

    _____

    _____

    _____

5. Who will the authentic audience for the product or service be?

    _____

    _____

    _____

HANDOUT 3.1C:
PRODUCT PLANNING GUIDE

ARTISTIC PRODUCTS

Architecture	Batik	Landscaping	Puzzles
Murals	Exhibits	Terrariums	Car designs
Decoration	Cartoons	Mosaic	Maps
Sculpture	Book covers	Collage	Sewing
Film strips	Costume	Silk screens	Puppets
Slideshows	Movies	Set design	Comic strips
Mobiles	Videos	Tinware	Yearbook
Aquariums	Pottery	Advertisements	Jewelry
Painting	Iron work	Drawing	Diorama
Webpages	Weaving	Graphic design	Furniture design
Package design	Calligraphy	Photography	Wood carvings
Postcards	Tessellations	Engraving	Political cartoons
Posters	Multimedia presentations	Etching	Horticultural design

PERFORMANCE PRODUCTS

Skits	Dance	Films	Interpretive dance
Role playing	Mime	Reader's theater	Simulations
Puppet shows	Poetry readings	Chorale	Plays
Monologues	Concerts	Stand-up comedy	Parades
Athletic events	Demonstrations	Improvisation	Reenactments

SPOKEN PRODUCTS

Debates	Lecture	D. J. shows	Book talks
Speeches	Mock trials	Panel discussions	Chronicles of important events
Radio plays	Songs	Celebrity roasts	Forums
Advertisements	Sales promotions	Narrations	Sign language
Storytelling	Demonstrations	Dedication ceremonies	Oral book reviews

Weather reports	Audiotapes	Interviews	Eulogies
Rap songs	Infomercials	Oral histories	Announcements
Newscasts	Comedy routines	Guided tours	Oral reports

WRITTEN PRODUCTS

Pamphlets	Parables	Analyses	Budgets
Brochures	Epics	Books	Laws
Web pages	Census reports	Graphs	Autobiographies
Folktales	Captions	Notes	Flow charts
Diaries	Amendments	Story problems	Poetry
Family trees	Public service announcements	Instructions	Marketing plans
Position statements	Ethnography	Interview questions	Outlines
Jokes/riddles	Timelines	Slogans	Letters/postcards
Recipes	Lyrics	Crossword puzzles	Discussion group questions
Legends	Questionnaires	Summaries	Limericks
Definitions	Invitations	Consumer reports	Grants
Bibliographies	Storyboards	Lists	Rhymes
Greeting cards	Magazine articles	Journal articles	Editorials

MODELS/CONSTRUCTION PRODUCTS

Drama sets	Gardens	Birdhouses	Instruments
Sculpture	Dioramas	Bulletin boards	Robots
Relief map	Shelters	Circuit boards	Machines
Habitat	Collections	Paper engineering	Rockets
Bridges	Ceremonies	Play facilities	Learning centers
Quilts	Food	Pottery	Computers
Multimedia presentation	Vehicles	Working models	Documentaries
Hydroponic farms	Fitness trails	Ant farms	Exhibitions Masks
Microscopes	Buildings	Toys	Aqueducts
Games	3-D figures	Catalogs	Mazes
Greenhouses	Solar collectors	Furniture	Blueprints

CATEGORY 4:
PUTTING KNOWLEDGE TO WORK

With general buy-in and a knowledge base created through the preceding activities, it is time to enlist volunteers who will put the program into action. Rather than appointing one leader, a team approach distributes the workload and incorporates more ideas and viewpoints. It is important to include those who might be more critical of the program as well as enthusiastic volunteers. Critics bring a valuable perspective to the table, and their presence encourages preemptive problem solving. We have found that including individuals from a variety of backgrounds—faculty, staff, administration, parents, and students—is key to developing a strong program in which all participants feel a sense of ownership. To develop a team, we suggest issuing invitations to potentially interested parties and strongly encouraging those who would be great members but hesitate to join. One way to encourage involvement is to offer suggestions for how various individuals with particular strengths might contribute to the effort (e.g., publicity, evaluation, scheduling, organization).

ACTIVITY 4.1
IDENTIFYING STEPS

Time: 45–60 minutes

Setting: Any group setting

Materials: Markers, chart paper

Designation: Required

Before beginning this activity, participants should have read Chapter 3: Seven Steps to Implementing a Cluster Program or a summary of the chapter. The facilitator should begin by reviewing each implementation step:

1. Learn about the interests of students and staff.
2. Set up a wall chart.
3. Create a schedule.
4. Locate facilitators.
5. Provide orientation for facilitators.
6. Register students for clusters that interest them.
7. Celebrate the success of the clusters.

After reviewing the steps, divide participants into seven groups, providing each with chart paper, and assign one of the seven steps to each. Ask the groups to generate ideas about how to address their step given site-specific information from their school. After approximately 10 minutes, ask groups to trade papers. Groups should read the notes of the previous group and add anything they believe will contribute to the discussion. Continue until all groups have had some time with each step. (After the initial 10 minutes for the first step, groups will need less time to add to previously worked on steps.) Once the steps are returned to their original group, ask each group to report on the most salient ideas for implementing the step. Encourage the group as a whole to discuss potential pitfalls that implementation might run into as well as possible solutions. Collect and compile the responses for the planning team to refer to as it begins implementation.

IDENTIFYING ROLES

Time: 10 minutes

Setting: Any group setting

Materials: Planning team

Designation: Optional

This meeting is best conducted after Activity 4.1: Identifying Steps. Participants should identify who will do the tasks identified in Activity 4.1: Identifying Steps and construct a timeline for accomplishing the tasks. (Issues raised in that activity might also give direction to the discussion.) It is best to encourage participants to choose jobs for which they are suited and that they want to do. The following four questions can guide the meeting:

1. What are the needs?
2. Who will do what?
3. What other information, resources, and training are needed?
4. What is an appropriate timeline for the identified tasks and items?

The team should develop a schedule of productive working sessions that may or may not include the entire team.

ACTIVITY 4.3
SETTING UP A WALL CHART

Time: 15 minutes

Setting: Any group setting

Materials: Wall chart, markers, chart paper

Designation: Recommended

Using the wall chart described in Chapter 3: Seven Steps to Implementing an Enrichment Cluster Program as an example, first discuss teacher and student interests, organize them by knowledge domain, and enter the information into the left side of the chart. Then brainstorm possible enrichment clusters that address the topics listed on the left side of the chart. Finally, ask participants to discuss how particular enrichment clusters might relate to and meet Common Core State Standards. (You may wish to refer participants to Table 2.1, which shows the Common Core State Standards met by Bill Bonfante's cluster, The Video Production Company.) Examining the CCSS helps participants see connections between cluster activities and the goals of "regular" school.

CATEGORY 5:
CREATING ONGOING SUPPORT

Once the program has been implemented and clusters are underway, professional development moves into a phase of ongoing support. Four specific components to ongoing staff development will help sustain continual improvement. First, program leaders need to provide orientation to people new to the program. Second, they need to establish a framework for the support, guidance, and encouragement necessary to move people from their initial offerings (which may resemble minicourses) to more authentic enrichment clusters. Third, they need to offer opportunities for reluctant staff to become involved. And fourth, they must set up a process that helps facilitators ensure that their clusters require students to access advanced content and authentic methodology and that assists them in using evaluation information to continually improve their clusters and the program as a whole.

PROVIDING ORIENTATION TO NEW PEOPLE

Schools see a constant influx of new people: new school faculty, students, parents, and community volunteers. As the enrichment cluster program develops, program leaders must bring new people on board in a systematic manner that provides them with the knowledge, background, and skills necessary to contribute to the program. Repeating some of the more formal in-service activities and providing materials such as this manual introduces new participants to the philosophy and methods behind an enrichment cluster program. Program leaders can also develop a materials packet that guides a mentor relationship with a new person. Each team member becomes responsible for new people as they are added to the enrichment program.

MOVING FACILITATORS FROM MINICOURSES TOWARD MORE AUTHENTIC CLUSTERS

Initially, enrichment clusters will vary from minicourses directed by the teacher to completely authentic enrichment clusters. No matter how thorough the start-up staff development sessions are, some facilitators will be less comfortable using an inductive, student-directed approach to teaching and learning than others. Providing a framework of continual support helps less comfortable teachers make the change in teaching style and develop more authentic clusters. A schoolwide celebration of excellent clusters will give teachers models that can be very helpful. In addition, staff development sessions in which facilitators evaluate their respective clusters can be an invaluable means of self-assessment and growth. The approach should always be to validate what has been done well and identify steps that will improve the next implementation. (Evaluating clusters in a group discussion encourages cluster facilitators to implement recommended improvements because they will not want to have to raise the same issues in subsequent evaluation sessions.)

INVOLVING RELUCTANT STAFF

When beginning a program, do not force anyone to facilitate a cluster; it will only breed animosity and resentment. Ideally, all staff would be involved in some manner with the program. Those who chose not to facilitate could assist other teachers or community volunteers. Reasons for not wanting to facilitate clusters range from opposition to the program to lack of confidence in being able to lead a cluster successfully. However, people can and do change their minds. Sometimes just sitting on the sidelines and watching someone facilitate is enough to make reluctant staff members want to try it themselves. Other times, interest increases after talking with students or colleagues about their experiences in clusters. Whatever the spark, it is important to keep the door open to people as they decide to come on board. Our experience with program implementation has shown that although initially only 60%–75% of faculty may choose to facilitate a cluster, after 3 years, often more than 95% of the faculty become involved and develop their own clusters. One method for encouraging involvement is to have enrichment program leaders offer personal invitations to individuals to develop a cluster. These invitations may be more attractive to some if they suggest the idea of team teaching or if they encourage participants to bring in special areas of interest or expertise.

FOCUSING ON ADVANCED CONTENT AND AUTHENTIC METHODS

One of the most effective means of helping facilitators incorporate advanced content and authentic methods into their clusters is to help them define these goals early in the program. In our pilot schools, we provided the Facilitator's Content/Methods Reporting Form (see Figure 5.1) in a folder at the outset of the cluster program to help facilitators keep track of how they address particular areas in their clusters. After a cluster block, it can serve as a checklist for program evaluation. A reproducible copy of Figure 5.1 appears in Handout 6f: Facilitator's Content/Methods Report, although schools may want to adapt it to meet their specific needs.

Another effective way to help facilitators incorporate advanced content and authentic methodology in their clusters is described in Activity 5.1: Efforts and Outcomes, in which facilitators debrief each other on what happened in their clusters. Before the cluster block is completed, we have also found that talking with facilitators helps them examine the vision and direction of their clusters. Having someone who clearly understands how to think outside the box by considering all the possible audiences, content, and outcomes for a particular cluster may help a

In your cluster, did you:	Yes/No	If "yes," please provide examples (use the reverse side if needed)
1. introduce new concepts and advanced content?	Y N	
2. help students develop a product or service?	Y N	
3. use advanced vocabulary related to the subject?	Y N	
4. teach specific, authentic methods?	Y N	
5. use authentic tools related to the topic?	Y N	
6. use advanced resources and reference materials?	Y N	
7. integrate advanced thinking and problem-solving strategies?	Y N	
8. encourage the use of creative thinking?	Y N	
9. help students create presentations or performances?	Y N	
10. encourage student-directed learning and choices?	Y N	
11. respond to student interests?	Y N	
12. involve students in hands-on activities?	Y N	
13. pose open-ended questions?	Y N	
14. integrate historical perspectives related to the content?	Y N	

FIGURE 5.1. Facilitator's content/methods reporting form.

facilitator move beyond the ordinary to the extraordinary. Consider the Sample Cluster A on volcanoes from Handout 2.2a: Someone intervening might encourage the cluster facilitator to determine what new or advanced content participants might learn by examining what a vulcanologist would study and how she would go about this study. Additionally, a program leader might suggest that the facilitator arrange for a guest speaker or consider having students build scale models of specific volcanoes, complete with classification concerning the type of volcano they had chosen to study. Students could develop historically accurate timelines of destruction for various volcanoes, make seismic predictions concerning future eruptions, create a global map of hot spots, or develop a relief awareness fund to benefit victims of volcanic displacement. Any of these suggestions would enhance this cluster.

ACTIVITY 5.1
EFFORTS AND OUTCOMES

Time: 30–45 minutes

Setting: Participants at tables

Materials: Handout 5.1: Efforts and Outcomes

Designation: Required

Invite all facilitators to a debriefing session to discuss their successes and plans for improvements. Create a celebratory atmosphere by awarding certificates and thank-you letters in this session and by offering food. Provide all facilitators with copies of Handout 5.1: Efforts and Outcomes. After giving participants some time to answer the questions on the handout, open up the session for discussion about how well they implemented the past enrichment cluster session. Encourage facilitators to share their successes and challenges, and to share what they saw their colleagues do well. Move the discussion toward the questions "What will you continue to do?" and "What will you change next time?" Collect the completed handouts for reference in subsequent debriefing sessions.

HANDOUT 5.1
EFFORTS AND OUTCOMES

Reflect on your cluster experience by answering the following questions:

1. In your cluster, in what manner were the following elements addressed?
   - Advanced Content

   _____
   _____
   _____

   - Authentic Methods

   _____
   _____
   _____

   - Product and/or Service

   _____
   _____
   _____

   - Authentic Audience

   _____
   _____
   _____

   - Student Driven

   _____
   _____
   _____

2. What do you believe you did exceptionally well?

_____

_____

_____

_____

_____

3. What would you do to improve this cluster in the future?

_____

_____

_____

_____

_____

CATEGORY 6:
USING EVALUATION DATA TO
IMPROVE THE PROGRAM

To ensure successful enrichment clusters, we suggest establishing a framework for ongoing evaluation. By continually monitoring progress and areas that need improvement, the program can build on its successes and correct its problems. We recommend beginning an enrichment cluster program with a short pilot series of clusters that lasts from 4–6 weeks. This pilot series can serve as the basis for adjustments and refinements that create a longer, more permanent schedule for the cluster program. Staff and student input and assistance in developing both the pilot and the permanent schedule will help build a successful program.

GATHERING EVALUATION DATA FROM STUDENTS

Evaluation from the students' perspectives is important because clusters are student centered and student driven. Such evaluation can range from simple to sophisticated, but whatever the complexity, it should only be used to improve the program on behalf of the students. Program leaders can gather student data using a variety of methods, such as observation, frequency of product development, interviews with a sample of students, and guided focus group discussions. In addition, program leaders can ask students to respond to simple evaluation forms, such as Handout 6a: Elementary Student Evaluation or Handout 6b: Secondary Student Evaluation. Students in third through eighth grade could complete a more sophisticated evaluation using an instrument such as "My Class Activities" (Gentry & Gable, 2001), which measures student attitudes toward their class activities on the constructs of challenge, choice, interest, and enjoyment. The results of this instrument can provide insights concerning how well the clusters addressed these constructs from a student's point of view. Facilitators should receive copies of student evaluation forms, as student comments will help them plan future clusters. No matter which method program leaders choose, it is important to build students' responses and productivity into an overall evaluation plan.

Because a major focus of enrichment clusters is to develop authentic products and services, we recommend assessing the quality of these outcomes. One instrument designed especially for this purpose is the Student Product Assessment Form (SPAF; Renzulli & Reis, 1997). This form is printed here for your use in Handout 6c: Student Product Assessment. It provides a valid and reliable means of assessing product quality as a measure of achievement. The SPAF includes two components. The first is related to the process of product development and includes eight items that have a Likert-type response format and a "not applicable" category. Each of these items is comprised of three parts: the key concept, a description of that item, and examples that help provide clarity. The second component of the SPAF is related to the overall quality of the products. It includes seven items with a 1–4 Likert-type response format. Copies of the summary sheet can be added to students' portfolios as a means of documenting their products. Both student evaluations and product assessment should be included in any formal program assessment report.

GATHERING EVALUATION DATA FROM FACILITATORS

When considering facilitator evaluation data, leaders should gather information in two areas. First, program leaders should find out how facilitators have reacted to the program, what their experiences were, and what they would suggest for improvement and additions to the program, including information on scheduling, topics, and how smoothly the program ran. Other considerations might include whether teachers or community volunteers would be willing to facilitate a cluster again in the future. To gather this information, we developed two evaluation forms, printed here as Handout 6d: Facilitator Evaluation and Feedback and Handout 6e: Cluster Reflections for Facilitators. Facilitators should complete these forms before group debriefing so that they won't be influenced by their colleagues.

Second, program leaders can compile information from facilitators concerning their use of advanced content and methods as well as the number and nature of products and services that students created. Leaders can then share this information with all facilitators to help them understand the scope of what young people can do and inspire them to develop engaging and challenging clusters in the future. For example, in the first implementation of enrichment clusters, leaders may find that only 60% of the clusters created a product or service. After sharing evaluation data suggesting that the session block was too short and sharing with facilitators examples of stellar clusters, leaders might extend the number of sessions and ultimately find that more than 90% produce a product or service in subsequent clusters. We recommend using the form in Handout 6f: Facilitator's Content/Methods Report to collect this information.

If the district has facilitators tying the clusters to Common Core State Standards, program leaders should compile a list of which clusters addressed which standards. Such information will provide needed justification of the importance of the program in terms of meeting and authentically reinforcing the district's adopted set of content standards and goals.

GATHERING EVALUATION DATA FROM PARENTS

In our research, we developed a parent survey (Reis, Gentry, & Park, 1995), printed here as Handout 6g: Parent Attitudes About Enrichment Opportunities, that assesses parent perceptions and satisfaction with enrichment opportunities in the school. This survey is especially useful in assessing whether the cluster program changes these parent perceptions of the school. Surveying the parents before and after the program can provide such information. If a school already uses existing parent surveys, we suggest adding questions about the enrichment cluster program to determine how parents view it. Responses can also provide insight into whether certain parents might like to become more involved in the program.

COMPLETE PROGRAM EVALUATION

It is important to develop an evaluation plan for the program. Program leaders, together with administration and the measurement/evaluation expert from the central office (if one is available), should determine what types of data to collect. This plan need not be complicated nor time-consuming, but it should be in place before the program starts. Evaluation will help determine what is working and what isn't. Far too often in education, programs are implemented without concern for evaluation, and participants and parents are left to wonder whether the program was effective. Without knowledge of outcomes—strengths and weaknesses—programs are left to whim. Using the data gathered from students, parents, and facilitators, leaders can develop an annual program evaluation report. This report should describe the program efforts, summarize the outcomes, explain the findings (including a section on strengths and another on weaknesses), and make recommendations for actions. At a minimum, the evaluation should include the following items:

- a summary of student evaluations,
- a summary of facilitator evaluations,
- the number of products and services completed,
- the audiences impacted by the products and services,
- the percentage of clusters and students involved in product or service completion, and
- a summary of the advanced content and methods used in the various clusters.

Other considerations include climate, discipline, and attendance data. (Our research and evaluation data has shown a decrease in discipline problems and an increase in attendance during the clusters.) The percentage of teachers who choose to facilitate a cluster is another informative piece of data that is very easy to collect. Again, our experience shows that over time more teachers will choose to become involved. Those who are initially reluctant to facilitate a cluster often do so as the program becomes part of the school culture. Whatever course the team chooses, evaluation is dynamic, should inform practice, and can be revised to gather information that the committee deems important.

ELEMENTARY STUDENT EVALUATION

Grade: _____ Cluster: _____

We would like to know how you feel about your experience in your enrichment cluster. Please read each statement carefully and circle the number that shows how you feel about each statement. A number 1 means that you agree with the statement. A number 2 means that you are not sure how you feel about the statement. A number 3 means that you disagree with the statement.

1. I enjoyed my cluster.   1 2 3

2. I learned new information/skills in my cluster.   1 2 3

3. My cluster teacher was interesting.   1 2 3

4. I am interested in participating in more enrichment clusters.   1 2 3

5. Please complete the following statements:
   a. I think an enrichment cluster should be offered on the following topic:

   _____

   b. One thing I learned in my enrichment cluster was:

   _____

   c. The thing I liked best about my enrichment cluster was:

   _____

   d. One change I would make to improve my enrichment cluster is:

   _____

HANDOUT 6B
SECONDARY STUDENT EVALUATION

Grade: _____ Cluster: _____

   We want to make our enrichment clusters even better, and we need your ideas. Please answer the questions below and tell us what you liked about your cluster. Please also describe what could be done to improve the clusters.

1. Did the clusters last too long, not long enough, or did they provide the adequate time to complete projects?

   _____
   _____
   _____
   _____
   _____

2. How might the cluster schedule be changed to make it better?

   _____
   _____
   _____
   _____
   _____

3. What did you like best about the clusters?

   _____
   _____
   _____
   _____
   _____

4. How can we make our enrichment cluster program even better?

_____

_____

_____

_____

_____

5. What did you learn in your cluster?

_____

_____

_____

_____

_____

6. If this cluster could continue, what else would you like to learn and do?

_____

_____

_____

_____

_____

7. What cluster topics do you suggest for next time?

_____

_____

_____

_____

_____

HANDOUT 6C

STUDENT PRODUCT ASSESSMENT

PART I: DIRECTIONS

RATIONALE UNDERLYING THIS ASSESSMENT FORM

The purpose of this form is to guide your judgment in the qualitative assessment of various types of products developed by students in enrichment programs. In using the instrument, three major considerations should always be kept in mind.

First, the evaluation of more complex and creative types of products is always a function of human judgment. We do not think in terms of percentiles or standard scores when we evaluate paintings, architectural designs, or the usefulness of a labor-saving device. We must consider these products in terms of our own values and certain characteristics that indicate the quality, aesthetics, utility, and function of the overall contribution. In other words, we must trust our own judgment and learn to rely upon our guided subjective opinions when making assessments about complex products.

A second consideration relates to the individual worth of the product as a function of the student's age, grade level, and experiential background. For example, a research project that reflects an advanced-level investigation and subsequent product by a first grader might not be considered an equally advanced level of involvement on the part of a sixth grader. Similarly, the work of a student from a disadvantaged background must be considered in light of the student's overall educational experiences, opportunities, and exposure to advanced-level resource persons, materials, and equipment.

The third consideration relates to the most important purpose of any evaluation—student growth and improvement. This assessment instrument should be used to guide students toward excellence, and, therefore, we strongly believe that it should be shared and discussed with students *before* the product is started. In other words, we believe the instrument should be reviewed with students during the early planning stages of the product. Students should have the opportunity to know and fully understand on what basis their final products will be assessed.

INSTRUCTIONS FOR USING THE ASSESSMENT FORM

Although most of the items included on the form relate directly to characteristics of the final product, it will also be helpful if you have access to planning devices that have been used in the development of the product. Such planning devices might include logs, contracts, management plans, proposals, or any other recordkeeping system. A planning device can help you to determine if prestated objectives have been met by comparing statements of objectives from the planning device with the final product. If such a planning device has not been used or is unavailable, you may want to request that students complete a form that will provide you with the necessary background information. It is recommended that some type of planning device accompany all products that are submitted for rating. If it can be arranged, you may also want to interview the student who completed the product.

In using this form, it will sometimes be necessary for you to do some detective work. For example, in determining the diversity of resources, you may need to examine footnotes, bibliographies or references, and materials listed on the planning device. You may also want to have the student complete a self-evaluation form relating to the completed product. This form may help to assess task commitment and student interest.

This form can be used in a variety of ways. Individual teachers, resource persons, or subject matter specialists can evaluate products independently or collectively as members of a team. When two or more persons evaluate the same product independently, the average rating for each scale item can be calculated and entered on the Summary Form. When used in a research setting or formal evaluation situation, it is recommended that products be independently evaluated by three raters. One of these ratings should be completed by the teacher under whose direction the product was developed. A second form should be completed by a person who has familiarity with the subject matter area of the product. For example, a high school science teacher might be asked to rate the work of an elementary student who has completed a science-related product. The third rater might be someone who is independent of the school system or program in which the work was carried out.

ITEM FORMAT

At first glance, the items on this form may seem long and complicated, but they are actually quite concise. Each item represents a single characteristic that is designed to focus your attention. The items are divided into the following three related parts:

1. *The Key Concept.* This concept is always presented first and is printed in large type. It should serve to focus your attention on the main idea or characteristic being evaluated.
2. *The Item Description.* Following the key concept are one or more descriptive statements about how the characteristic might be reflected in the student's product. These statements are listed under the key concept.
3. *Examples.* In order to help clarify the meanings of the items, an actual example of student work is provided. The examples are intended to

elaborate upon the meaning of both the key concept and the item description. The examples are presented following each item description.

Important note: The last item (No. 9) deals with an overall assessment of the product. In this case, we have chosen a somewhat different format, and examples have not been provided. When completing the ratings for Item No. 9, you should consider the product as a whole (globally) rather than evaluating its separate components in an analytic fashion.

Some of the items may appear to be unusually long or detailed for a rating scale, but our purpose here is to improve the clarity and thus the interrater reliability for the respective items. After you have used the scales a few times, you will probably only need to read the key concepts and item descriptions in order to refresh your memory about the meaning of an item. Research has shown interrater reliability is improved when items are more descriptive and when brief examples are provided in order to help clarify any misunderstanding that may exist on the parts of different raters.

"NOT APPLICABLE" ITEMS

Because of the difficulty of developing a single instrument that will be universally applicable to all types of products, occasionally there will be instances when some of the items do not apply to specific products. For example, in a creative writing project (e.g., poem, play, story), either the Level of Resources (No. 3) or Diversity of Resources (No. 4) might not apply if the student is writing directly from his or her own experiences and imagination. It should be emphasized, however, that the "Not Applicable" category should be used very rarely in most rating situations.

HOW TO RATE STUDENT PRODUCTS

1. Fill out the information requested at the top of the Summary Sheet that accompanies this form. A separate Summary Sheet should be filled out for each product to be evaluated.

2. Review the nine items on the form. This review will help to give you a "mindset" for the things you will be looking for as you examine each product.

3. Examine the product by first doing a quick overview of the entire piece of work. Then do a careful and detailed examination of the product. Note pages or places that you might want to reexamine and jot down brief comments about any strengths, weaknesses, or questions that occur as you review the product.

4. Turn to the first item on the form. Read the key concept, item description, and example. Enter the number that best represents your assessment in the "Rating" column on the Summary Sheet. Enter only whole numbers. In other words, do not enter ratings of 3.5 or 2.25. On those rare occasions when you feel an item does not apply, please check the NA column on the Summary Sheet. Please note that we have only included an NA response option for Item 9a on the Overall Assessment.

5. Turn to the second item and repeat the above process. If you feel you cannot render a judgment immediately, skip the item and return to it at a later time. Upon completion of the assessment process, you should have entered a number (or a check in the NA column) for all items on the Summary Sheet.

6. Any comments you would like to make about the product can be entered at the bottom of the Summary Sheet.

HANDOUT 6C
STUDENT PRODUCT ASSESSMENT

PART II: SUMMARY SHEET

Name(s): _____ Date: _____

District: _____ School: _____

Teacher: _____ Grade: _____ Sex: _____

Product (Title and/or Brief Description):

_____

_____

Number of Weeks Student(s) Worked on Product: _____

RATING SCALES
Factors 1–8
5 – To a great extent
3 – Somewhat
1 – To a limited extent

Factors 9A–9G
5 = Outstanding
4 = Above Average
3 = Average
2 = Below Average
1 = Poor

Factors	Rating	Not Applicable
1. Early Statement of Purpose		
2. Problem Focusing		
3. Level of Resources		
4. Diversity of Resources		
5. Appropriateness of Resources		
6. Logic, Sequence, and Transition		
7. Action Orientation		

Factors	Rating	Not Applicable
8. Audience		
9. Overall Assessment		
A. Originality of the Idea		
B. Achieved Objectives Stated in Plan		
C. Advanced Familiarity with Subject		
D. Quality Beyond Age/Grade Level		
E. Care, Attention to Details, etc.		
F. Time, Effort, Energy		
G. Original Contribution		

Comments:

_____

_____

Person Completing This Form _____

1. EARLY STATEMENT OF PURPOSE

Is the purpose (theme, thesis, research question) readily apparent in the early stages of the student's product? In other words, did the student define the topic or problem in such a manner that a clear understanding about the nature of the product emerges shortly after a review of the material?

For example, in a research project dealing with skunks of northwestern Connecticut completed by a first-grade student, the overall purpose and scope of the product are readily apparent after reading the introductory paragraphs.

5	4	3	2	1
To a great extent		Somewhat		To a limited extent

2. PROBLEM FOCUSING

Did the student focus or clearly define the topic so that it represents a relatively specific problem within a larger area of study?

For example, a study of "Drama in Elizabethan England" is more focused than "A Study of Drama."

5	4	3	2	1
To a great extent		Somewhat		To a limited extent

3. **LEVEL OF RESOURCES**

    Is there evidence that the student used resource materials or equipment that are more advanced, technical, or complex than materials ordinarily used by students at this age/grade level?

    For example, a sixth-grade student utilizes a nearby university library to locate information about the history of clowns in the 12th–16th centuries in the major European countries.

5	4	3	2	1
To a great extent		Somewhat		To a limited extent

4. **DIVERSITY OF RESOURCES**

    Has the student made an effort to use several different types of resource materials in the development of the product? Has the student used any of the following information sources in addition to the standard use of encyclopedias: textbooks, record/statistic books, biographies, how-to books, periodicals, films and film strips, letters, phone calls, personal interviews, surveys or polls, catalogs, and/or others?

    For example, a fourth-grade student interested in the weapons and vehicles used in World War II reads several adult-level books on this subject, including biographies, autobiographies, periodicals, and record books. He also conducts oral history interviews with local veterans of World War II, previews films and film strips about the period, and collects letters from elderly citizens sent to them from their sons stationed overseas.

5	4	3	2	1
To a great extent		Somewhat		To a limited extent

5. **APPROPRIATENESS OF RESOURCES**

    Did the student select appropriate reference materials, resource persons, or equipment for the topic or area of study?

    For example, a student who is interested in why so much food is thrown away in the school cafeteria contacts state officials to learn about state requirements and regulations that govern what must and can be served in public school cafeterias. With the aid of her teacher, she also locates resource books on how to design, conduct, and analyze a survey.

5	4	3	2	1
To a great extent		Somewhat		To a limited extent

6. **LOGIC, SEQUENCE, AND TRANSITION**

    Does the product reflect a logical sequence of steps or events that ordinarily would be followed when carrying out an investigation in this area of study? Are the ideas presented clearly and logically, and is there a smooth transition from one idea or subtopic to another?

For example, a student decides to investigate whether or not a section of his city needs a new fire station with a salaried staff rather than the present volunteer staff. First, the student researches different methods of investigative reporting such as appropriate interview skills. Next, the student conducts interviews with both salaried and volunteer fire station staff. He then learns about methods of survey design and reporting in order to analyze local resident opposition or support for the new fire station. After other logical steps in his research are completed, his accumulated findings lead him to interviews with the mayor and the board of safety in the city and then to several construction companies that specialize in bids on such buildings. His final product is an editorial in the local newspaper that reflects his research and conclusions.

5	4	3	2	1
To a great extent		Somewhat		To a limited extent

7. ACTION ORIENTATION

Is it clear that the major goal of this study was for purposes other than merely reporting on or reproducing existing information, ideas, or knowledge? In other words, the student's purpose is clearly directed toward some kind of action (e.g., teaching ways to improve bicycle safety, presenting a lecture on salt pond life); some type of literary or artistic product (e.g., poem, painting, costume design); a scientific device or research study (e.g., building a robot, measuring plant growth as a function of controlled heat, light, and moisture); or some type of leadership or managerial endeavor (e.g., editing a newspaper, producing/directing a movie).

For example, a student decides to study the history of his city. After an extensive investigation, the student realizes that other history books have been written about the city. He finds, instead, that no one has ever isolated specific spots of historical significance in the city which are easily located and accessible. He begins this task and decides to focus his research to produce an original historical walking tour of the city.

5	4	3	2	1
To a great extent		Somewhat		To a limited extent

8. AUDIENCE

Is an appropriate audience specified or readily apparent in the product or management plan?

For example, the student who researched the history of his city to produce an original walking tour presents his tour to the city council and the mayor. They, in turn, adopt it as the official walking tour of the city. It is reproduced in the city newspaper and distributed by the local historical society and library, and given out to registered guests in the city's hotels and motels.

5	4	3	2	1
To a great extent		Somewhat		To a limited extent

9. OVERALL ASSESSMENT
Considering the product as a whole, provide a general rating for each of the following factors and mark the space provided to the right of the item:

RATING SCALE
5 = Outstanding
4 = Above Average
3 = Average
2 = Below Average
1 = Poor

A. Originality of the idea. _____
B. Achieved objectives stated in plan. _____
C. Reflects advanced familiarity (for age) with the subject matter. _____
D. Reflects a level of quality beyond what is normally expected of a student of this age and grade. _____
E. Reflects care, attention to detail, and overall pride on the part of the student. _____

HANDOUT 6D
FACILITATOR EVALUATION AND FEEDBACK

Name (Optional): _____

Your feedback and input are essential to the success of the enrichment cluster program. By taking a few minutes to complete the evaluation questions below, you will be assisting us in improving and further developing the program for your students.

1. What did you enjoy most about facilitating your cluster?

    _____

    _____

    _____

    _____

    _____

2. Were the clusters well organized? How can the program be changed or improved?

    _____

    _____

    _____

    _____

    _____

3. What were the students' reactions to your cluster?

    _____

    _____

    _____

    _____

    _____

4. What types of advanced content did you present in your cluster?

_____

_____

_____

_____

_____

5. What products (if any) were produced by students in your cluster?

_____

_____

_____

_____

_____

6. Are you interested in facilitating another cluster? Yes / No
   If yes, what topic(s)?

_____

_____

_____

_____

7. Can you recommend other potential facilitators and possible topics for the next session?

_____

_____

_____

_____

8. What recommendations would you make for scheduling the clusters (i.e., how many sessions, length of sessions)?

    _____

    _____

    _____

    _____

    _____

9. Other comments:

    _____

    _____

    _____

    _____

    _____

    Thank you!

HANDOUT 6E

CLUSTER REFLECTIONS
FOR FACILITATORS

Please complete this evaluation to assist us in the improvement of our enrichment cluster program.

Thank you for all your devotion, time, and talent. You have helped make our program a success!

Name of cluster you facilitated: _____

You are (circle one): School Faculty / Staff Member / Volunteer

1. Was the cluster schedule adequate? How might the schedule be improved?

   _____

   _____

   _____

   _____

   _____

2. How can the enrichment cluster program be improved?

   _____

   _____

   _____

   _____

3. Do you think the cluster ran smoothly? How could the organization be improved?

   _____

   _____

   _____

   _____

4. What did you like best about facilitating your cluster?

_____

_____

_____

_____

_____

5. What did you learn in your cluster?

_____

_____

_____

_____

_____

6. Did you think the students enjoyed the clusters?

_____

_____

_____

_____

_____

7. Did you think the students benefited from the cluster?

_____

_____

_____

_____

_____

8. Did you enjoy the cluster?

_____

_____

_____

_____

_____

9. Did you benefit from the cluster?

   _____

   _____

   _____

   _____

   _____

10. Can you suggest possible cluster topics for the spring?

    _____

    _____

    _____

    _____

    _____

11. Additional comments or concerns:

    _____

    _____

    _____

    _____

    _____

Thank you!

HANDOUT 6F
FACILITATOR'S CONTENT/ METHODS REPORT

Please circle "yes" or "no" for the following questions, providing examples on the lines given for all "yes" answers.

In your cluster, did you . . .

1. Introduce new concepts and advanced content? Yes / No

   _____

   _____

   _____

2. Help students develop a product or service? Yes / No

   _____

   _____

   _____

3. Use advanced vocabulary related to the subject? Yes / No

   _____

   _____

   _____

4. Teach specific, authentic methods? Yes / No

   _____

   _____

   _____

5. Use authentic "tools" related to the topic? Yes / No

   _____

   _____

   _____

6. Use advanced resources and reference materials? Yes / No

_____

_____

_____

7. Integrate advanced thinking and problem-solving strategies? Yes / No

_____

_____

_____

8. Encourage the use of creative thinking? Yes / No

_____

_____

_____

9. Help students create presentations or performances? Yes / No

_____

_____

_____

10. Encourage student-directed learning and choices? Yes / No

_____

_____

_____

11. Respond to student interests? Yes / No

_____

_____

_____

12. Involve students in hands-on activities? Yes / No

_____

_____

_____

13. Pose open-ended questions? Yes / No

_____

_____

_____

14. Integrate historical perspectives related to the content? Yes / No

_____

_____

_____

PARENT ATTITUDES ABOUT ENRICHMENT OPPORTUNITIES

Name: _____ Child's Name: _____

Child's Grade: _____

I am the child's _____Mother _____Father _____Guardian

Following are 10 statements. Please respond to them by circling the number that best represents your answer, using the following scale:

5=Always   4=Often   3=Sometimes   2=Seldom   1=Never

For the purposes of this questionnaire, *enrichment experiences* are defined as planned opportunities beyond regular classroom work designed to extend and add depth to your child's education. Examples include speakers, videos, and interest-based activities.

1. My child has opportunities for enrichment experiences in school.	5 4 3 2 1
2. During school, my child is encouraged to develop and pursue his or her talents.	5 4 3 2 1
3. My child develops projects in the classroom that reflect her or his interests.	5 4 3 2 1
4. My child has opportunities to work with other students in his or her classroom who share common interests.	5 4 3 2 1
5. My child's school offers enrichment opportunities for all students.	5 4 3 2 1
6. My child enjoys the enrichment opportunities in his or her school or classroom.	5 4 3 2 1
7. My child is happy about attending school.	5 4 3 2 1
8. I am informed about the educational enrichment activities for my child at school.	5 4 3 2 1
9. I have the opportunity to become involved with enrichment opportunities in school.	5 4 3 2 1
10. I am satisfied with enrichment experiences my child receives at school.	5 4 3 2 1

Please comment briefly on the following items:

1. What do you like most about your child's school experience?

   _____

   _____

   _____

   _____

   _____

2. What changes would you like to see made regarding your child's school or classroom experiences?

   _____

   _____

   _____

   _____

   _____

3. Please provide other comments that will help us understand your attitude toward school and satisfaction with your child's experience in his or her classroom or school.

   _____

   _____

   _____

   _____

6

RESEARCH UNDERLYING THE ENRICHMENT CLUSTER PROGRAM

Build a powerful case.

—Perry Mason

We have been field testing and fine-tuning the enrichment clusters programming model for many years. This chapter summarizes what we have learned from our comparative (Gentry, Moran, Reis, Renzulli, & Warren, 1995; Reis & Gentry, 1998; Reis, Gentry, & Park, 1995) and evaluative studies on enrichment clusters in both urban and suburban districts and schools. We have implemented enrichment clusters in small and large schools, in schools with outstanding administrative and faculty support and in those with more limited support. The schools we have used as pilots have also had a range of levels of financial support. In all sites, we used both quantitative and qualitative methodologies in this research and evaluation. Quantitative methods included descriptive procedures, and qualitative procedures included observations, interviews, and questionnaire data gathered through participant observation (Spradley, 1980). We coded field notes, interview transcripts, document reviews, and all other collected data and analyzed them for patterns and themes. The coding process used combined techniques described by Spradley (1979, 1980) and by Strauss and Corbin (1990). The following results have emerged from our work in investigating enrichment clusters with respect to the categories of program success, student effects, parent attitudes, and effects on teacher practices.

PROGRAM SUCCESS

1. It was possible to successfully implement enrichment clusters in a wide variety of schools, including rural, suburban, and urban areas, as well as in low socioeconomic areas and in culturally diverse settings.

2. Across all of these schools, clusters were adapted and tailored to fit individual school schedules and needs. Our experience revealed that more than 90% of the schools that implement clusters continue the program, making improvements as the program develops.

3. Schools that have implemented clusters often serve as model sites for other school districts that are considering implementing clusters.

4. Despite initial concerns, we have consistently found that cross-age grouping by interest works well in enrichment clusters. Up to a span of four grades, age differences are not apparent when children are grouped by common interest. There are exceptions if clusters require skills that children may not have attained, such as writing.

5. Community members in all pilot schools were actively involved on a regular basis through enrichment clusters. Different forms of community involvement included the integration of programs such as artists in residence, school to work, and business/school partnerships.

6. It was possible to set aside time during the school week when the focus was on student and teacher interests, when students had choices, and when there was challenge and enjoyment in learning. The range of programming times in the sites we studied varied from a 60-minute time block once a week to 4 half-days per week, with the majority of schools setting aside 90 minutes once a week. The number of weeks per cluster session ranged from 6 weeks to the entire school year. Many schools offered several cluster sessions, each 6–12 weeks long, throughout the school year.

7. Total schoolwide enrichment could be provided, and gifted education pedagogy was successfully extended to students of all achievement levels.

8. Students with special needs and special education personnel were actively and productively involved in enrichment clusters in all sites.

STUDENT EFFECTS

1. After enrichment clusters were implemented, students involved in the clusters displayed stronger interests than students not involved in clusters. Girls in the experimental group showed stronger interests in language arts than girls in the comparison group; boys in the experimental group showed stronger interests in math and science than boys in the comparison group.

2. Attendance was higher on enrichment cluster days, both for students and for teachers, than on noncluster days, suggesting that school was an attractive place to be on cluster days.

3. Approximately 90% of the students completed group or individual products in clusters, and there were no differences in the number of products produced when examined by achievement, gender, special program placement, or ethnicity. With regard to the development of products or services, a majority of the cluster facilitators in both schools used student products and services as the outcome of the clusters. Overall, in 80% of the clusters offered during the pilot and treatment sessions, students developed products, performances, and services. In every cluster that ran for 12 weeks (School A) or 10 weeks (School B), students developed products. In the shorter pilot series of only three sessions, student products were developed in 85% of the clusters in School A and in 71% of the clusters in School B. These findings suggest that if clusters are offered over longer periods of time, it is more likely that student products and services would result.

The development of products and services provides further evidence of the use of advanced content in the clusters. Students in The Paleontology Association researched attributes of dinosaurs, developed their own dig, wrote research proposals, discovered a new dinosaur using the content that they had learned, named and described their new dinosaur based upon its attributes and adaptations to the environment from which it came, and presented their findings in an analytical research paper during a mock scientific forum. The teacher who assisted the professionals who facilitated this cluster explained: "At first I thought that the materials and the expectations of the facilitators were beyond the students' capabilities, yet as the cluster continued, I was amazed at how well students did with the advanced nature of the cluster." She indicated that students were able to take advantage of resources such as videos, artifacts, articles, and actual paleontologists. At the conclusion of the cluster, the teacher observed that "The quality of the students' work was truly extraordinary, and their products were very advanced for second through fifth grade students."

4. Upon examining student products, we found no differences in quality among various achievement levels. This finding suggests that when students with common interests work together to develop a product, achievement levels do not appear to predict the quality of the products.

5. After 3 years in the enrichment cluster program, one middle school saw increases in student proficiency as measured by their state mastery exams in all subject areas (reading, math, language, science, social studies).

PARENT ATTITUDES

In one study (Reis, Gentry, & Park, 1995), parents in both of the treatment schools held improved perceptions about enrichment opportunities after the implementation of the cluster program. Parents' perceptions about enrichment and their satisfaction with enrichment increased from the beginning of the year to the end.

EFFECTS ON TEACHER PRACTICES

1. The majority of teachers enjoyed facilitating clusters. In the four schools from which we collected long-term evaluation data, initial staff involvement in cluster facilitation averaged 60%. After 2 program years, the average had increased to more than 90%. At one middle school, 60% of the teachers indicated that they wanted more time to devote to the clusters after an initial 8-week implementation. At an elementary site, 32 of 34 teachers indicated after their first attempt at facilitating an enrichment cluster that they strongly wished to facilitate another.

The most positive reactions about facilitating a cluster came from those teachers who had chosen to pursue an interest of their own in a cluster. Often these topics had nothing to do with teachers' regular classroom activities. One art teacher assisted with a cluster in the fall, but then decided to facilitate her own cluster in the spring because she had an interest in computers. She admitted that this second cluster was a more exciting experience for her. Other teachers became increasingly positive and more relaxed as the year continued.

We asked for feedback from all facilitators after both the fall and spring series in order to modify the program to accommodate the schools' needs. Almost every teacher recognized the overwhelming interest in and excitement for clusters by students and saw tremendous value in the program. We found in our research that teachers who facilitated or assisted with clusters began to use strategies from enrichment clusters in their regular classrooms. (Teachers had not been requested to modify practices in their classrooms as a part of the study.) When asked if enrichment clusters influenced what occurred in their classrooms with respect to either methods or content, 13 out of 22 teachers in School A and 8 out of 14 teachers in School B indicated that strategies they employed or learned while facilitating enrichment clusters carried over into their classroom. In all, almost 60% of the teachers said that clusters had influenced what they currently do in their classrooms. Because more than half of the teachers indicated that they had voluntarily changed their teaching as a result of this involvement, the use of enrichment clusters seems very promising as a professional development strategy.

After determining whether each classroom teacher believed that the clusters had influenced teaching practices in their classrooms, we examined the ways in which teachers said they modified their classrooms and teaching as a result of their involvement in the clusters. Specifically, the influences of enrichment clusters on classroom practices fell into two categories: content and teaching methods.

CONTENT

Eighty-six percent of the teachers who reported that clusters influenced their classrooms indicated the influence had been in the area of content, including areas such as developing centers related to cluster content, integrating cluster content into classroom curriculum and lessons, and using ideas and community resources gained from the clusters in the classroom. Across both sites, out of 21 teachers who indicated that the enrichment clusters had affected their classroom teaching, three teachers reported that they had developed and used interest centers as a direct result of their work with the clusters, nine teachers reported that they integrated cluster content into their classrooms, and four said that they had involved community members and outside resources they had worked with while facilitating clusters in their classrooms. The facilitator for the History of the Motion Picture cluster explained, "We developed an interest center for the library that was filled with the old movies we studied in the cluster. Students from the cluster and others from the school who heard about the cluster or who had an interest in old movies could check out the movies and watch them at home." As a result, he influenced students in other classrooms as well as his own. Similarly, an art teacher reported that she was able to take advantage of student interest generated in clusters in her regular art classes and build upon art concepts that students learned in clusters: "Students in the cluster were so excited about what they were learning that it was a logical extension to integrate things like calligraphy and drawing into the regular art curriculum." Further, three other teachers stated that the enrichment clusters had influenced the content in their classrooms because students brought back ideas and knowledge that they could integrate into their classes. For example, students who had been working online in their technology cluster shared their web quests with their classmates, and showed them how to become involved in several online data projects. Although enrichment clusters are designed to focus on student and teacher interests and not necessarily relate to the prescribed curriculum, our analysis indicated that they had a positive impact upon the content and curriculum in the classrooms for more than half of the teachers who participated in this study.

TEACHING METHODS

Enrichment clusters also influenced teaching methods, with 86% of the teachers who reported that clusters had influenced their classrooms indicating that the influence had been in the area of teaching methods. These teachers reported an increase in their use of the following strategies within their classrooms:

- responding to student interests,
- using hands-on activities,
- encouraging student-directed learning and choices,
- using interest groups in the classroom,
- encouraging students to complete products and independent work, and
- increasing concentration on thinking skills.

Nine out of 21 teachers reported that they had learned to encourage students to pursue interests more in their classrooms. One teacher explained, "After working in the clusters, I felt more free to offer students options based on their interests . . . I also think that the students were more likely to want to take off in directions of their choosing." Not only did these teachers learn more about the students' interests, but they also reported that students learned more about the teachers' interests, which provided a more personally meaningful educational experience for both. Teachers reported using interests as a basis for lessons and projects as well as for grouping children within their classrooms. Four teachers said that they use hands-on activities such as experiments, building, videotaping, acting, and dioramas as well as student exploration more often than before the clusters. They reported using these activities because their students enjoyed being active and seemed to learn more when working with hands-on activities, as they had done in most of the enrichment clusters.

Encouraging student direction and choice was reported by five teachers. These teachers tried to facilitate rather than teach by promoting choice of projects, allowing choice of group members (often those with similar interests), and encouraging choice of roles within the classroom. Three teachers reported that they used interest groups in their classrooms that centered around a project or theme. Teachers reported that grouping by interest worked so well in the clusters that it was a logical extension to continue to use it in their classrooms.

Six teachers reported encouraging students to develop products and projects and to work independently. These teachers reported that their students seemed to be excited about their projects from the clusters, so they decided to integrate more opportunities for student-chosen products and projects in their classrooms. One teacher said that instead of assigning book reports, she gave students the option of developing products related to their language arts readings. As a result, students developed critiques, commercials, videos, skits, and advertisements related to their reading assignments, all of which the teacher reported were of high quality. The spillover of cluster-type products into the regular classroom was a positive outcome of teachers' involvement with the enrichment clusters.

Two teachers indicated that they also concentrated more on thinking skills, including problem solving and critical and creative thinking. One teacher indicated that she was amazed at the advanced level of the work and thinking within her cluster: "I was surprised by how motivated the students were to tackle the difficult concepts that were presented to them in this cluster. Some of my own students were in the cluster, and after watching them in that setting, I've decided to expect more from them in class. The hands-on nature of the cluster coupled with the higher order processes were motivating to my students." Table 6.1 shows a summary of the content and methods used by teachers in their classrooms.

Whereas 58% of the teachers indicated that the clusters had directly influenced their classrooms, another 42% indicated that their teaching had not been directly changed. Yet, several of these teachers qualified this response. Some teachers said that the enrichment clusters were too new and therefore had not yet influenced what they do in their classrooms, while another teacher said that the clusters did not influence her work in the classroom because of current curricular constraints. Others believed they had been teaching like cluster facilitators for years and that it was "nice to have the opportunity to focus on this type of teaching and not have to hide it." In sum, of the 15 teachers who said that the enrichment clusters had not influenced their classroom content or teaching methods, five qualified their remarks.

Teachers used advanced content and methodologies in the enrichment clusters and provided challenges and choices to students. The types of advanced content and the frequency of use are depicted in Table 6.2, followed by an explanation of how advanced content and methods were used.

USE OF ADVANCED CONTENT, METHODS, AND PROCESSES

Ninety-five percent of the cluster facilitators indicated that they used new, advanced concepts. For example, students in the language clusters (e.g., Sign Language, The French League, The Spanish Group, The Latin Association) learned new words in the language, as well as information about the customs and lifestyles of people from other cultures. Science clusters (e.g., Paleontologist Society, Young Scientists, SOS Project Recycle, Engineering I, Snakes in the Grass, Bluebirds, Forest and Wildlife Biologists, Invention Convention) covered content rarely found in traditional elementary curricula. These clusters dealt authentically with how scientists work, and the students assumed the roles of inventors, biologists,

TABLE 6.1
ENRICHMENT CLUSTER CONTENT AND METHODS USED BY TEACHERS IN THEIR CLASSROOMS

(N = 21 teachers)

Content Description	Percentage of Teachers
Integration of cluster content into classroom curriculum and lessons	43
Use of ideas and community resources gained from clusters	19
Development of centers related to enrichment cluster content	14
Responding to student interests	43
Encouraging student-directed learning and choices	24
Encouraging students to complete products and independent work	29
Using hands-on activities	19
Using interest groups in the classroom	14
Increasing concentration on thinking skills	14

TABLE 6.2
ADVANCED CONTENT AND METHODOLOGIES IN CLUSTERS BY PERCENTAGE OF USE

(N = 121 clusters)

Strategy	Percentage of Clusters Using Strategy
1. Introduction of new concepts and advanced content	95
2. Development of product or service	81
3. Teaching specific, authentic methodologies	81
4. Use of advanced vocabulary	65
5. Use of authentic tools related to the topic	56
6. Use of advanced resources and reference material	53
7. Use of advanced thinking and problem-solving strategies	44
8. Integration of creative thinking	43
9. Integration of historical perspectives	24
10. Development of presentations or performances	13
11. No advanced content used	5

conservationists, or paleontologists. The inventors designed plans and developed prototypes of their ideas, and the biologists obtained a baseline of the flora and fauna that existed on school property. Dance and movement clusters (e.g., Spring Training, Creative Dance Troupe, Tap Dance Association, These Boots Were Made for Walking) introduced the cultural influence of dance as well as new steps and the impact of exercise on the body. Students in clusters that focused on writing (e.g., Young Authors, School Newspaper, History of the Motion Picture, Poets Society) learned new genres of writing as well as techniques for brainstorming, writing, and editing.

Students in 65% of the clusters learned advanced vocabulary. Students in The Horticultural Society and The Horticultural Alliance learned Latin names for plants, parts of the plants, the concept of germination, and many other terms that professionals involved with horticulture and landscaping use on a regular basis. The resources for both of these clusters were at a reading level above most of the students, yet the students were able to handle the vocabulary and the Latin because of their specific interest in the topic. (During one observation, a student in this cluster asked another student if she could go get the *ilex subulata* so that she could plant it before its root stock dried out.) Vocabulary, when it is meaningful and tied to student interests, can challenge the students to learn beyond what might be expected at their "level."

Another area that emerged in the analysis of advanced content use was the integration of historical perspectives within the context of the cluster. Approximately 24% of the facilitators reported that they had addressed the history of the content area of their clusters. Students learning how to sign reviewed the history of sign languages to provide a better perspective on their existence and development today. Students involved in The Paleontologists' Society examined earth history and theories of extinction, and students in The Latin Association looked at the history of language and culture as they discovered Latin as a root of modern language. The integration of history within the clusters offered students opportunities to uncover the roots of knowledge disciplines while learning new techniques and concepts related to their chosen areas of interest. Historical perspectives provided authentic grounding in many clusters.

The use of specific, authentic methodologies in many clusters provides further evidence of their advanced nature. Children in Capture the Spirit learned how to use a camera to create photographic essays. Students in the Invention Convention learned how to identify a problem, suggest solutions, develop their ideas, propose solutions on paper first, and then build a prototype of their actual invention—just as professional inventors do. Students in the Police Academy and Detectives clusters learned how to interview witnesses, document evidence, and take fingerprints in order to solve crimes. Students in clusters that included performance or production aspects learned how to prepare and perform in front of an audience, much as real actors, musicians, puppeteers, and dancers do. Approximately 75% of the clusters provided evidence of integrating authentic methodologies related to the cluster topics.

In addition, the introduction and use of tools needed to accomplish tasks within the cluster emerged as evidence of authentic methodology. Facilitators in more than half of the clusters had students use tools specific to cluster topics and tasks. These tools were specific to the nature of the cluster and allowed students to perform or act like practicing professionals within the interest area addressed by the cluster. Students in Invention Convention learned to use drafting equipment to make scale drawings of their inventions and saws and hammers to construct them. Students in Young Entrepreneurs, Young Reporters, and Talent Productions learned to use computers, design copy, and develop and lay out advertising. Photographers and videographers learned to use the camera, camcorder, and editing equipment. In Spring Training, students used stethoscopes, heart monitors, and other equipment to measure body fat and blood pressure.

Facilitators in 55% of the clusters used advanced resources and reference materials with the students, including videos, cassettes, magazines, slides, online computers, films, technical papers, artifacts, centers, blueprints, books, speakers, and field trips to challenge students and capture their interests. After assessing what students wanted to draw, the Young Artists facilitator brought in examples of work by artists and the needed equipment, such as quill pens and ink, French curves, calligraphy pens, and sketching pencils, which experts then demonstrated to the students. The facilitator stated that using authentic resources such as experts, equipment, and the sample work from artists was not possible within the regular art curriculum due to time and space constraints. She reported that as a result of this in-depth exposure, the students in the cluster were able to work at a much more advanced level.

Several clusters (13%) employed performances and presentations, which usually required the use of advanced methodology or content. Some of the performances were for large audiences and others for individual classrooms, but all reflected the work and pride of the children involved. Students in several clusters, such as Creative Dance Troupe, performed original dances that they had developed and choreographed for their schools, and two of their routines became part of talent show performances for larger audiences during the evening. Students in the puppetry clusters developed their own puppets, wrote their own scripts, and produced a puppet show for their classmates, parents, and teachers.

Advanced thinking, problem solving, and creative thinking were also evident in many of the enrichment clusters. Forty-four percent of the cluster facilitators reported that students used advanced thinking and problem solving, and 43% of the facilitators reported that students used creative thinking during cluster sessions. Students in History of the Motion Picture used critical thinking to write movie reviews. Additionally, they used creative thinking when they developed promotional posters for the movies they viewed. In The Horticultural Society, students had to use creative thinking skills in order to conceive and develop a landscape plan for the entrance to the school.

Enrichment clusters served as an effective means of professional development. In our pilot sites, the initial amount of formal professional development that accompanied the implementation of clusters was limited to an hour at the beginning of the year. The real professional development occurred in the work setting. Teachers worked with each other, with community members, with university researchers, and with students to practice a new way of teaching. The more time that teachers had to work on their clusters and to experiment with this inductive way of teaching, the more advanced the content and the more diverse the products and services became. Based on previous findings of classroom practices studies by Archambault et al. (1993) and Westberg, Archambault, Dobyns, and Salvin (1993), it would appear that the experience of teaching in a cluster program greatly increases a teacher's use of differentiation strategies in their own classroom teaching situations, and, correspondingly, leads to more advanced learning opportunities. Enrichment clusters may then serve dual purposes: exciting learning opportunities for all children and new models for teacher professional development in differentiation strategies and enrichment.

Our research indicated that faculty who participate in an activity such as enrichment clusters in which they have an opportunity to practice innovative teaching methods that enhance student learning will transfer these skills to their own classrooms. In contrast to professional development programs that take the form of "professional development days," this cluster program was organized with minimal effort and costs.

In some schools, the professional development program that began in clusters actually continued to expand with very little input from program leaders. In one of our pilot schools, the enrichment coordinator (and enrichment cluster program leader for the school) was a very positive and upbeat person who continually thanked teachers for their participation and offered to help them in any way possible. As the year continued, a group of teachers approached the enrichment coordinator and asked about working with her to develop other enrichment opportunities. Together, they started a schoolwide enrichment team, one of the recommended strategies in *The Schoolwide Enrichment Model* (Renzulli & Reis, 2014). The purpose of the team was to make recommendations about enrichment opportunities and develop a more organized approach to schoolwide enrichment. The team was open to any interested staff members, included the principal and two parents, and represented a range of grades. Based on feedback from students and teachers, the assembled group adopted a proposal, which was approved by the principal, to set aside an afternoon block each week for enrichment clusters. The change that occurred in this school resulted from a team effort, not from the administrative leaders alone.

IMPLICATIONS

Like a garden that flourishes, spilling over its edges, the enrichment cluster programs implemented in pilot schools spread beyond their initial frames. Teachers brought methodology and content learned in clusters to their regular classrooms, and students worked on cluster-like projects on their own at home or sought out teachers who shared special interests. One art teacher said she looked forward to doing clusters again because she felt she was able to expose many students to things that they normally wouldn't be able to do within the curriculum. She had many students come to her for help after the clusters were over or bring her things they had created on their own.

The majority of the staff at both pilot schools believed that the enrichment clusters were a positive addition to the school and chose to schedule clusters for the following year. Schools with established enrichment cluster programs served as models for other schools that were interested in beginning a cluster program as a way to implement one component of the Schoolwide Enrichment Model. Due to reports in area newspapers, news of the cluster program spread and similar programs were implemented in other schools. At least seven districts modeled their new cluster program on visits to the two urban districts that participated in this research.

These cluster programs were organized with little effort or cost, and the greatest challenge to implementing the program was finding a common block of time for all teachers and students to participate in the program. Enrichment clusters have great potential to provide student-driven, high-end learning to all students, and our research has shown many benefits to students and their teachers. An education in which students focus on their strengths, interests, and talents, applying them to real-world products and services for authentic audiences, ought to be expected for our youth and their teachers. Enrichment clusters are an exciting way of delivering on the promise to help each child reach his or her fullest potential.

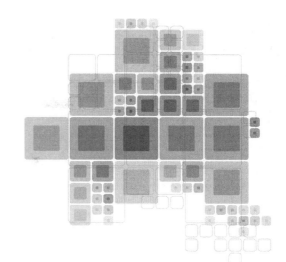

REFERENCES

Archambault, F. X., Jr., Westberg, K. L., Brown, S. W., Hallmark, B. W., Emmons, C. L., & Zhang, W. (1993). *Regular classroom practices with gifted students: Results of a national survey of classroom teachers* (Research Monograph No. 93102). Storrs: University of Connecticut, The National Research Center of the Gifted and Talented.

Baum, S., Gable, R., & List, K. (1987). *Chi square pie charts and me.* Unionville, NY: Royal Fireworks Press.

Burns, D. E. (1992). If I ran the school. Author.

Darling-Hammond, L. (1997). *The right to learn: A blueprint for creating schools that work.* San Francisco, CA: Jossey-Bass.

Darling-Hammond, L. (2009). Recognizing and enhancing teacher effectiveness. *International Journal of Educational and Psychological Assessment, 3,* 1–24.

Dewey, J. (1939). *Education and experience.* New York, NY: Collier.

Fulton, L. (Ed.). (2002). *The directory of poetry publishers.* Paradise, CA: Dustbooks.

Gentry, M., & Gable, R. K. (2001). My class activities: A survey instrument to assess students' perception of interest, challenge, choice, and enjoyment in their classrooms. West Lafayette, Indiana: Gifted Education Resource Institute, Purdue University.

Gentry, M., Moran, C., Reis, S. M., Renzulli, J. S., & Warren, L. (1995). *Enrichment clusters: Using high-end learning to develop talents in all students.* Storrs: University of Connecticut, The National Research Center on the Gifted and Talented.

Gentry, M., Reis, S. M., & Moran, C. (1999). Expanding program opportunities to all students: The story of one school. *Gifted Child Today, 2*(4), 36–48.

Gentry, M., & Renzulli, J. S. (1995). Inspiration: Targeting my ideal teaching situation. Storrs: University of Connecticut, The National Research Center on the Gifted and Talented.

Gottschalk, L. (1969). *Understanding history: A primer of historical method.* New York, NY: Alfred A. Knopf.

Ingersoll, R., & Perda, D. (2010). *How high is teacher turnover and is it a problem?* Philadelphia: University of Pennsylvania, Consortium for Policy Research in Education.

Karnes, F. (2014). *The best competitions for talented kids: Win scholarships, big prize money, and recognition.* Waco, TX: Prufrock Press.

Kettle, K. E., Renzulli, J. S., & Rizza, M. G. (1998). Products of the mind: Exploring student preferences for product development using My Way . . . An Expression Style Inventory. *Gifted Child Quarterly, 42,* 48–61.

Purcell, J. H., & Renzulli, J. S. (1998). *Total talent portfolio: A systematic plan to identify and nurture gifts and talents.* Waco, TX: Prufrock Press.

Ravitch, D. (2010). *The death and life of the great American school system: How testing and choice are undermining education.* New York, NY: Basic Books.

Reis, S. M., & Gentry, M. (1998). The application of enrichment clusters to teachers' classroom practices. *Journal for the Education of the Gifted, 21*(3), 310–334.

Reis, S. M., Gentry, M., & Park, S. (1995). *Extending the pedagogy of gifted education to all students* (Research Monograph No. 95118). Storrs: University of Connecticut, The National Research Center on the Gifted and Talented.

Renzulli, J. S. (1994). *Schools for talent development: A comprehensive plan for total school improvement.* Waco, TX: Prufrock Press.

Renzulli, J. S. (1997). *Interest-A-Lyzer family of instruments: A manual for teachers.* Waco, TX: Prufrock Press.

Renzulli, J. S., & Reis, S. M. (1997). *The schoolwide enrichment model: A comprehensive plan for educational excellence (2nd ed.).* Waco, TX: Prufrock Press.

Renzulli, J. S., & Reis, S. M. (2014). *The schoolwide enrichment model: A comprehensive plan for educational excellence (3rd ed.).* Waco, TX: Prufrock Press.

Schack, G. D., & Starko, A. J. (1998). *Research comes alive! Guidebook for conducting original research with middle and high school students.* Waco, TX: Prufrock Press.

Spradley, J. P. (1979). *The ethnographic interview.* New York, NY: Holt, Rinehart and Winston.

Spradley, J. P. (1980). *Participant observation.* New York, NY: Holt, Rinehart and Winston.

Starko, A. J., & Schack, G. D. (1992). *Looking for data in all the right places: A guidebook for conducting original research with young investigators.* Waco, TX: Prufrock Press.

Strauss, A. L., & Corbin, J. (1990). *Basics of qualitative research: Grounded theory, procedures and techniques.* Newbury Park, CA: Sage.

Treffinger, D., Isaksen, S., & Dorval, B. (2000). *Creative Problem Solving: An Introduction (3rd ed.).* Sarasota, FL: Center for Creative Learning.

Westberg, K. L., Archambault, F. X., Jr., Dobyns, S., & Salvin, T. (1993). *An observational study of instructional and curricular practices used with gifted and talented students in regular classrooms* (Research Monograph No. 93104). Storrs: University of Connecticut, The National Research Center on the Gifted and Talented.

APPENDIX A

IF I RAN THE SCHOOL SURVEY

Developed by Deborah E. Burns

Name _____

Grade _____   Teacher _____

I am really interested in:

SCIENCE

1. The Stars and Planets
2. Birds
3. Dinosaurs and Fossils
4. Life in the Ocean
5. Trees, Plants, and Flowers
6. The Human Body
7. Monsters and Mysteries
8. Animals and Their Homes
9. Outer Space, Astronauts, and Rockets
10. The Weather
11. Electricity, Light, and Energy
12. Volcanoes and Earthquakes
13. Insects
14. Reptiles
15. Rocks and Minerals
16. Machines and Engines
17. Diseases and Medicine
18. Chemistry and Experiments

ENRICHMENT CLUSTERS

SOCIAL STUDIES
1. Families
2. The Future
3. Our Presidents
4. The United States
5. Other Countries
6. History and Long Ago Times
7. Famous Men and Women
8. Problems We Have in Our Town
9. Holidays
10. Native Americans, Asian Americans, Hispanics, and African Americans
11. Explorers
12. People Who Live and Work in Our Town
13. Travel and Transportation

MATH
1. Math Games and Puzzlers
2. Measuring Lines, Liquids, Weight
3. Shapes and Sizes
4. Buying and Money
5. Calculators and Computers
6. Building
7. Counting and Numbering
8. Calendars and Time
9. Math Stories and Problems

LANGUAGE ARTS
1. Writing a Book
2. Writing Poems
3. Writing Plays and Skits
4. Writing Newspapers
5. Making Speeches
6. Sign Language
7. Making a Book
8. Comic and Cartoon Strips
9. Letter Writing
10. Spanish and French
11. Talking and Listening to Stories
12. Making a New Game or Puzzle

ARTS

1. Cartoons
2. Art Projects
3. Painting
4. Clay
5. Acting
6. Dancing
7. Drawing
8. Writing Music
9. Photography
10. Movies
11. Puppets
12. Radio and Television
13. Famous Artists and Their Work
14. Making New Toys
15. Magic
16. Mime

CAREERS

1. Doctors
2. Lawyers
3. Police Work
4. Firefighters
5. Scientists
6. Builders
7. Reporters
8. Store Workers
9. Sports Stars
10. Actors
11. Veterinarians
12. Farmers
13. Writers
14. Engineers
15. Artists
16. Inventors

You forgot to list some of my very special interests. They are:

_____

_____

_____

APPENDIX B

SAMPLE ENRICHMENT CLUSTER DESCRIPTIONS

Following are examples of real clusters that took place in schools involved in our research studies. We have organized them by the general interest areas identified in the sample wall chart in Chapter 3 (Figure 3.2). Some include facilitator bios, which is optional.

LANGUAGE ARTS, LITERATURE, AND THE HUMANITIES

THE POETS' WORKSHOP

What is it like to be a poet? Explore the poetry of some of America's greatest poets, including Robert Frost, Langston Hughes, Emily Dickinson, and others. Write, illustrate, and perform original poems or interpret others' work. Identify outlets for our work.

VOICES FROM OLYMPUS

Step back into the lives of an ancient civilization. Was the world held on the shoulders of a giant? Did monsters lurk in the depths of a maze? Was the world controlled from a mountain top? Let's explore the world of the ancient Greeks. What connections can we make to our world today?

AMERICAN SIGN LANGUAGE

How do people communicate without using a voice? In this cluster, American Sign Language will be introduced through both words and songs. Decide what to do with your newfound language. Who might be your audience?

YOUNG AUTHORS GUILD

Are you an aspiring writer? Join other writers in creating original works in any genre you choose, such as poetry, fiction, drama, and short story. Help identify outlets for your work. Submit for publication, enter contests, create a performance, develop a gathering of writers, and more.

PHYSICAL AND LIFE SCIENCES

INVENTION CONVENTION

Are you an inventive thinker? Would you like to be? Come to this cluster to brainstorm a problem, try to identify many solutions, and design an invention to solve the problem. Create your invention individually or with a partner under the guidance of Bob Erickson and his colleagues. You may share your final product at the Young Inventor's Fair, a statewide, daylong celebration of creativity.

HABITAT HUNTERS

Have you ever wondered why penguins live at the South Pole? Why plants and animals live where they do? Will your children know the same plants and animals you do? How are plants and animals in our area currently affected by human population and expansion? What can we do to save these species from extinction? Make a difference: Join the Habitat Hunters as we explore these issues and more.

FLIGHT SCHOOL

Pilot your own helicopter! Discover how and why a glider flies and build one to test your ideas. Construct a rubber-powered model airplane and launch your own rocket to understand more about Bernoulli's Principle and Newton's Third Law. Discover the history of flight and the science of simple machines. You will be able to plan and complete your own project and experience one of life's greatest rewards, "taking two steps back to admire your own work." Mr. Schimmel is a former teacher, director of an environmental education center, and currently a school administrator in Mansfield. He obtained his pilot's license in 1981 and continues to enjoy learning about why and how bats, birds, and boomerangs—as well as numerous man-made machines—manage to FLY! Mrs. Latino is a fourth-grade teacher at Southeast School who has a variety of interests, including skiing and sailing.

HERPETOLOGISTS' SOCIETY: REPTILE DISCOVERY

Explore the mysteries, superstitions, myths, and real-life problems for reptiles in today's world. Get up close and personal with reptile specimens. Discover what issues herpetologists study, identify how you can make a difference in the world of reptiles, and then take action.

PALEONTOLOGIST SOCIETY

Step back in time to the Jurassic era. Explore the lost world of the dinosaurs with staff from Dinosaur State Park. Explore geologic time, invertebrate fossils, fossil plants, and fossilization, and work beside paleontologists as you explore the mysteries of the past at the dig site. Decide what to create as a result of your work.

THE ARTS

ANIME CADRE

Do you like to draw? Are you fascinated by the Japanese art of anime and manga? If so, join us as we explore the history of anime—and try your hand at drawing your own anime characters. We will create a futuristic setting and an elaborate plot together as a group and then let our characters explore this new world together.

PRINTING WITH PANACHE!

Explore printmaking by creating your own print "blocks." Use different printing techniques, such as the "rainbow roll," to create your own art. Take a look at early printmaking techniques, body prints, vegetable prints, and monoprint techniques. Your artistic productions will be worthy of framing and more. Help decide appropriate outlets for this exciting work.

CREATIVE PUPPETRY

So you want to be a puppeteer? Come design and create several different kinds of puppets, such as finger puppets, hand puppets, marionettes, and more. Experiment with and develop your own character. Write, direct, or star in a puppet show by bringing your puppets to life in a performance. The stage and your imagination are the only limits.

CARTOONING

Doodle, draw, and dabble in the life of comic strip artists and cartoonists. This cluster is for both new and experienced illustrators, artists, and cartoonists. Come prepared to turn on your imagination and creativity. Create your own comical characters and produce a comic strip series for syndication in our crazy comic club, or submit your work for publication in another outlet. Samantha Dunnack is a well-read fan of the funnies.

JUST CLOWNING AROUND

Become a clown and develop an original clown character that suits just you. Use costuming, makeup, funny hats, and accessories to create your own unique clown look. Learn to make balloon animals and prepare a program or skit that might become a school or community presentation.

THE CHIMERS: A HANDBELL CHOIR

Do you love music? Become a member of the cluster handbell choir, learn the techniques associated with this type of music, and play, compose, and prepare for authentic performances.

SOCIAL SCIENCES

CREATIVE PROBLEMS, CREATIVE SOLUTIONS

Are you interested in becoming involved in the community? Do you have a desire to help others? Identify various problems in our communities or lives and solve them using creative problem solving. Apply creative problem solving to other situations and create and enact your solutions.

CHILDREN'S RIGHTS' INSTITUTE

"That's not fair!" Have these words ever come out of your mouth? What is the difference between whining and real problems? What are the rights of people under 18 years old? Explore laws that define how you live and how they may be different from the laws that determine how other kids live. Develop a plan for action.

CULTURAL CONCOCTIONS

Why did Middle Eastern tribes develop a taste for lambs' eyes, while the Asian subcontinent smacked their lips over steamed monkey brains? Explore culture, genetics, and survival. Who survives and why?

MATHEMATICS

SURVEY SAID . . .

Do you want to find out what people think about things? Survey your friends, your family, or the community about something you've always wanted to know. Organize their responses in a creative way. Decide how to share this information. Develop and conduct a survey and communicate your results in this exciting enrichment cluster.

NUMBERS, MATHEMATICS, AND GAMES

Come create, produce, and play game with mathematics. What makes a good game and how have games been used in education and in cultures? What can be done with new games? Explore these questions and more on your quest to develop the next game that everyone is talking about.

BOLD FOLDS

Can paper frogs jump? Explore this and other questions in a cluster about the Chinese art of Origami. Research the history of Origami and find out how it is used today. Connect Origami to geometry. Produce you own 3-dimensional figures out of paper by practicing with existing designs or designing and creating your own! Decide what can be done today with Origami.

COMPUTERS AND TECHNOLOGY

ROBOT CHALLENGE

Interested in robots? Ever want to design and build your own robot? How do robots work and how are they used? Come explore what robots can do now and in the future.

VIDEO PRODUCTION

Become a moviemaker and produce a video for a box office audience. Show your creativity and movie-making panache through the camera lens and on the big screen. Learn tricks and techniques of the trade while developing your film.

WEBSITE DESIGNERS

Are you interested in website design? Explore the how, what, and why of web design. Sharpen your skills and determine a product or service and begin creating. Work alone or with a design team.

APP BUILDERS WORKSHOP

Are you addicted to your iPhone or iPad, and do you want to learn how to create your own apps for these devices? Explore the app building process from concept to design to publishing. By the end of the workshop you will impress your friends with a fully-functioning app that you can share with others!

CACHE CHASERS

Are you a treasure hunter at heart? Do you like playing hide and seek? If so, geocaching is for you. In this cluster you will hide objects for others to uncover and discover how to find hidden objects using handheld GPS units. Join the growing community of geocachers around the globe.

GRAPHIC NOVEL SOCIETY

If you have seen all the recent superhero movies, or if you automatically flip to the comics section of the newspaper on Saturday morning, the Graphic Novel Society is for you! You will create comics and graphic novels using computer software and free websites available online. Hone your drawing abilities and get ready to explore a world where anything can happen.

PHYSICAL EDUCATION

CULTURAL STOMPERS INSTITUTE

In this cluster, you will be able to design an interactive process that will facilitate cultural diversity and rhythmic stomping movements. You can use your skills to design costumes or develop different and unique steps. Create community performances, workshops, and beyond.

CREATIVE MOVEMENT

Are you tired of being told to stay still and sit down? Express your inner self through creative movement! Be you! Step out of the limits! Step out of the box and find out there is no box!

GYMNASTICS

Develop important gymnastic skills, movements, and tricks. Use a variety of gymnastic equipment and plan a routine for your gymnastic performance.

SPRING TRAINING

Come try activities designed to enhance your total body awareness. Discover how to use your mind to become more skillful, fit, and knowledgeable about your physical abilities. Brainstorm and determine ways to have an impact on ourselves and others who may not have an interest in personal fitness. Personal trainers and physical education teachers Dr. Michael Gerich and Kelli MacFarlane will guide you through this cluster.

FAMILY AND CONSUMER SCIENCES

CULINARY ARTS INSTITUTES

Is cooking and eating your thing? How does a chef differ from a cook? What makes good food great? Join Chef Roger in a culinary journey. Develop skills and identify products and services to which to apply your love of cooking and eating. The kitchen is big!

HABITAT FOR HUMANITY

Are you interested in construction and tools as well as making a difference in the community? If so, this cluster is for you. Join Habitat for Humanity in our town as we work to develop livable residences for elderly and needy residents.

APPENDIX C

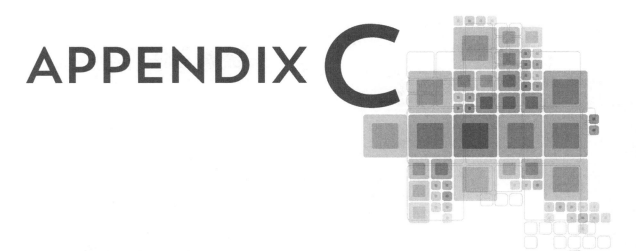

METHODOLOGICAL RESOURCES

REAL-WORLD RESEARCH SKILLS

Square Pie Charts and Me by Susan Baum, Robert Gable, and Karen List (Unionville, NY: Royal Fireworks Press, 1987)

Designed to help adults teach children how to become original researchers, this resource addresses topics such as the research process, types of research, management plans, presentation of studies, and statistical techniques.

Action Research for Kids: Units That Help Kids Create Change in Their Community by Amanda O. Latz, Ed.D., and Cheryll M. Adams, Ph.D. (Waco, TX: Prufrock Press, 2013)

Action Research for Kids provides teachers with comprehensive, creative, and hands-on units to engage students in action research. Students will benefit from learning about quantitative and qualitative research practices that can make a real difference in their lives and those within their communities. Within this text, teachers can select a lesson or use whole units as students explore research methods such as survey research, experimental research, life history, and photovoice in fun lessons that ask them to create a library wish list, interview people in their communities, lobby for cookies in the cafeteria, and experiment with preservatives. Each lesson comes with detailed instructions and ideas for differentiation.

Looking for Data in All the Right Places: A Guidebook for Conducting Original Research With Young Investigators by Alane J. Starko and Gina D. Schack (Waco, TX: Prufrock Press, 1992)

Get elementary school students out of the library and into the real world! Teachers can use this excellent guidebook to help their students learn how to gather and analyze data in order to answer their research questions. Each user-friendly chapter includes explanations, examples, and practice activities for different steps of the research process.

Research Comes Alive! by Gina D. Schack and Alane J. Starko (Waco, TX: Prufrock Press, 1998)

This comprehensive guide to conducting research with middle and high school students covers how to develop research questions, types of research, data-gathering techniques, how to analyze and interpret data, and outlets for sharing information. Activities help students practice skills.

Statistics for Kids: Model Eliciting Activities to Investigate Concepts in Statistics by Scott A. Chamberlin, Ph.D. (Waco, TX: Prufrock Press, 2013)

Perhaps the most useful and neglected content area of mathematics is statistics, especially for students in grades 4–6. In this book, teachers will facilitate learning using model-eliciting activities (MEAs), problem-solving tasks created by mathematics educators to encourage students to investigate concepts in mathematics through the creation of mathematical models. Students will explore statistical concepts including trends, spread of data, standard deviation, variability, correlation, sampling, and more—all of which are designed around topics of interest to students.

Exploring People and Cultures: Authentic Ethnographic Research in the Classroom by Mary Ellen Sweeney, Ph.D., and Brooke Walker, Ph.D. (Waco, TX: Prufrock Press, 2012)

This book provides teachers with tools and activities for conducting a classroom study of ethnic groups and cultures. Through the more than 30 ready-to-use, differentiated lessons, teachers will help students to learn how to recognize the elements of culture; think critically; apply real-world research techniques in field experiences; identify behavior patterns in modern-day cultures; and create, plan, and share their products in a student-led ethnography fair.

HOW-TO TITLES

A Teen's Guide to Getting Published: Publishing for Profit, Recognition, and Academic Success (2nd ed.) by Jessica Dunn and Danielle Dunn (Waco, TX: Prufrock Press, 2006)

This revised edition, written by two successful former teen authors, offers practical writing tips and an expansive listing of print and online markets that publish student work. It provides concrete advice, encouragement, and motivation to young authors looking to make their mark, addressing topics including the writing craft, freelance writing, rights and copyright information, publishing pitfalls, writing camps and workshops, and staff writing and book publishing.

A Teen's Guide to Creating Web Pages and Blogs by Benjamin Selfridge, Peter Selfridge, and Jennifer Osburn (Waco, TX: Prufrock Press, 2009)

Whether using a social networking site like MySpace or Facebook, or building a web page from scratch, millions of teens are actively creating a vibrant part of the Internet. This is the definitive teen's guide to publishing exciting web pages and blogs. This book leads readers step by step through the basics of HTML and web design, with an inquisitive approach that encourages experimentation and fun. Students will learn to go beyond clicking through websites to learning strategies for web design, including placing and editing images, linking to other sites, creating multipage sites, incorporating various font styles, and using JavaScript to create advanced homepages.

Animation Unleashed: 100 Principles Any Animator, Comic Book Writer, Filmmaker, Video Artist, and Game Developer Should Know by Ellen Besen (Studio City, CA: Michael Wiese Productions, 2008)

Animation's potential as a powerful tool for communication is just beginning to be understood. This book reveals key principles, useful for both professionals and beginners, that will help you harness the full power of this exciting and ever-expanding medium.

Go: A Kidd's Guide to Graphic Design by Chip Kidd (New York, NY: Workman, 2013)

This book is a stunning introduction to the ways in which a designer communicates his or her ideas to the world. Chip Kidd is "the closest thing to a rock star" in the design world (*USA Today*), and in *Go* he explains not just the elements of design, including form, line, color, scale, typography, and more, but most important, how to use those elements in creative ways. The book ends with 10 projects.

Art Is Every Day: Activities for the Home, Park, Museum, and City by Eileen S. Prince (Chicago, IL: Chicago Review Press, 2012)

An art project and activity book aimed at helping children and adults improve their basic understanding of art, this reference stresses art elements and principles, which in turn promote observation and discovery on a daily basis. Ideal for anyone wanting to bring meaningful, rich, and fun art experiences into children's lives, this work is stocked with 65 artsy activities for the home, park, city, or even museum. Projects include going on a photographic scavenger hunt in search of forms and shapes, writing an imaginary autobiography based solely on a museum portrait, and making a sand castle on a trip to the beach. The projects, which are accessible and require only free or inexpensive materials, are accompanied by a helpful index that categorizes projects by elements and principles.

American Folk Art for Kids by Richard Panchyk (Chicago, IL: Chicago Review Press, 2004)

Drawing on the natural folk art tendencies of children, who love to collect buttons, bottle caps, shells, and popsicle sticks to create beautiful, imperfect art, this activity guide teaches kids about the history of this organic art and offers inspiration for them to create their own masterpieces. The full breadth of American folk art is surveyed, including painting, sculpture, decorative arts, and textiles from the 17th century through today. Making bubble gum wrapper chains, rag dolls, bottle cap sculptures, decoupage boxes, and folk paintings are just a few of the activities designed to bring out the artist in every child. Along the way kids learn about the lives of Americans throughout history and their casual relationships to everyday art as they cut stencils, sew needlepoint samplers, draw calligraphy birds, and design quilts.

Break A Leg: The Kid's Guide to Acting and Stagecraft by Lise Friedman (New York, NY: Workman Publishing, 2001)

Young performers learn warm-ups, stretches, and breathing exercises to hone body and voice; discover theatre games and improvisations; develop essential skills from clowning to enacting a death scene; and turn within to create vivid characters. A 16-page insert on costumes and make-up; a backstage tour of props, drops, pits, and rigging; plus advice on coaches, agents, and going professional round out this great resource.

The Art of Construction: Projects and Principles for Beginning Engineers and Architects by Mario Salvadori (Chicago, IL: Chicago Review Press, 2000)

Using historical examples from caves to skyscrapers, this resource takes students through the principles of engineering and architecture. Project suggestions using household items give students a hands-on understanding of all aspects of structure and design.

Engineering the City: How Infrastructure Works by Matthys Levy and Richard Panchyk (Chicago, IL: Chicago Review Press, 2000)

Discover the fascinating story of infrastructure, from power lines and bridges to sewers and tunnels. Experiments, projects, and construction diagrams show how these essential but often invisible structures are built, how they work, and how they affect the environment of the city and the land around it.

Climbing Your Family Tree: Online and Off-line Genealogy for Kids by Ira Wolfman (New York, NY: Workman Publishing, 2001)

Filled with comprehensive information on using the Internet, *Climbing Your Family Tree* shows children how to dig up family documents, ships' manifests, naturalization papers, and birth, marriage, and death certificates. Readers learn how to create oral histories, detail a family tree, and make a scrapbook of family lore.

Hands-On Archaeology: Real-Life Activities for Kids (Rev. ed.) by John R. White, Ph.D. (Waco, TX: Prufrock Press, 2005)

Written by renowned archaeologist John White, this book shows any teacher or parent how to help kids become young archaeologists. Of equal importance is that while learning the discipline, students will be acquiring skills in math, biology, geology, art, geography, history, and language, as well as motor, social, and conceptual skills. From creating simulated archaeology, to participating in digs in the classroom, to digs in the community, students will not just learn about archaeology—they will be archaeologists!

Filmmaking for Teens: Pulling Your Shorts Off (2nd ed.) by Troy Lanier and Clay Nichols (Studio City, CA: Michael Wiese Productions, 2010)

By applying the tools in this book, young filmmakers can learn everything they need to know about how to make a great short film. The updated edition of this classic manual includes numerous additions reflecting the enormous changes impacting the world of digital video.

Screenwriting for Teens: The 100 Principles of Screenwriting Every Budding Writer Must Know by Christina Hamlett (Studio City, CA: Michael Wiese Productions, 2006)

This books gives teens—who go to the movies more than any age group in the world—the tools to write their own films. Concepts covered include plot, pacing, character development, and introductions to various genres.

Creating History Documentaries: A Step-by-Step Guide to Video Projects in the Classroom by Deborah Escobar (Waco, TX: Prufrock Press, 2001)

Learn how to integrate historical photos, film footage, interviews, and primary-source materials to create real-world projects to share with students, parents, and community members! Students research using the newest tools, write narrative scripts around historical facts, and build a project that brings history alive. Also included is how-to information on video cameras, computer software, online research, sources of historical photos and video footage, and more.

Public Speaking: 7 Steps to Writing and Delivering a Great Speech by Katherine Pebley O'Neal (Waco, TX: Prufrock Press, 2008)

Students can learn how to organize information into a presentation that will interest and amaze their classmates. They will discover exciting ways to start a speech and lots of intelligent techniques to use in the middle to keep the audience attentive. Here they will discover tricks to keep from getting nervous, and special, easy ways to remember what to say. Using these new skills, your students will be entertaining, informative, and confident.

Speak Out! Debate and Public Speaking in the Middle Grades by Kate Shuster and John Meany (New York, NY: International Debate Education Association, 2005)

This book is a primer for beginning and intermediate students participating in class and contest debates. Combining the practical and theoretical, it teaches students the basics of public speaking, argumentation, and research.

The Kids' Book of Weather Forecasting by Mark Breem and Kathleen Friestad (Charlotte, VT: Ideals, 2008)

No matter which way the wind blows, kids will be observing and predicting with their new knowledge of the weather. Youngsters learn about meteorology as they build weather stations from scratch, keep weather logs to record observations, create graphs and charts to spot weather trends, and explore how hurricane, tornado, blizzard, and flood predictions are becoming more accurate.

The Kids' Guide to Digital Photography: How to Shoot, Save, Play With, and Print Your Digital Photos (Rev. ed.) by Jenni Bidner (New York, NY: Sterling, 2011)

This comprehensive, popular beginner's guide for kids is now reissued with updated information and photos. Fun, easy to follow, and visually appealing, it teaches young photographers how to create, edit, and share their digital images in imaginative ways—from using basic features like the zoom and flash to changing color, removing red eye, and using the finished photos in cool projects. Sidebars simplify concepts like megapixels and megabytes, and the book includes a glossary.

Making Handmade Books: 100+ Bindings, Structures, and Forms by Alisa Golden (Asheville, NC: Lark Crafts, 2011)

In the digital world, books may seem like an endangered species, but bookmaking is more popular than ever. Thanks to the 100 ideas in this volume, the craft is now available to everyone. In as little as an afternoon, beginners will be on their way to folding, gluing, and sewing handmade books in a variety of shapes and styles, from rolled scrolls to Jacob's ladders, folded flexagons to case bindings. Complete with photographs of the author's own master books and statements by more than 40 established book artists, this collection is sure to inspire.

Making Shadow Puppets by Jill Bryant, Catherine Heard, and Laura Watson (Buffalo, NY: Kids Can Press, 2002)

Based on puppet designs from around the world, projects include a list of materials, step-by-step instructions, and colorful illustrations. Readers explore the history of shadow puppets as well as traditional characters and materials used. Also included are instructions for making a box screen and doorway screen and suggestions for lighting, props and scenery, writing a script, assigning roles, and practicing.

The Complete Book of Marionettes by Mabel and Les Beaton (Mineola, NY: Dover, 2011)

This instructive and engaging guide, written by professionals with a passion for their art, provides everyone from beginners to veteran performers with all the information needed to create these beloved figures and the stages on which they perform. Enhanced with more than 200 sequenced photographs and diagrams, the comprehensive manual contains valuable advice for making heads, bodies, wigs, and puppet clothing and includes entire chapters on how to manipulate the puppet, set up and furnish a stage, light scenes, and even how to build miniature pieces of furniture. A production chapter tells how to incorporate music, put on sketches, parody celebrities, and arrange programs. There's even a complete script for *Beauty and the Beast*, as well as a section on the history of puppeteering.

Model Making by Martha Sutherland (New York, NY: W. W. Norton & Co., 1999)

Using readily available materials such as paper, illustration board, foam core, and balsa wood, students can construct scale models of their dream house, community park ideas, or set designs. Easy-to-follow instructions help young architects, artists, and engineers transfer paper renderings into 3-D models in order to study design or present ideas to an audience.

Origami Inspired by Japanese Prints by Steve and Megumi Biddle (London, England: British Museum Press, 2012)

A reissue of this popular book with a gorgeous new cover design that unfolds to reveal 48 brightly colored double-sided sheets of origami paper. This book includes materials and illustrated instructions for making a range of origami creations from birds to flowers, animals to insects, all inspired by Japanese masters such as Hiroshige, Utamaro, and Hokusai.

Philosophy for Kids: 40 Fun Questions That Help You Wonder About Everything! by David A. White, Ph.D. (Waco, TX: Prufrock Press, 2001)

This innovative resource introduces kids to the world of philosophy and philosophers. Arranged by topic (values, knowledge, reality, and critical thinking), activities ask students to explore concepts and relate them to today's issues ("Do we control technology or does technology control us?"). In addition to learning about a challenging subject, students will sharpen their ability to think critically about these and similar questions. Experiencing the enjoyment of philosophical thought enhances a young person's appreciation for the importance of reasoning throughout the traditional curriculum of subjects.

Real Life Math Mysteries by Mary Ford Washington (Waco, TX: Prufrock Press, 1995)

An assistant city engineer poses a problem with runoff water drainage; an architectural estimator needs to determine the cost of constructing a building; a fire fighter must figure how fast to pump water on a fire to extinguish it. Students learn real-world application of important math skills while also learning about a variety of careers.

The Science of Life: Projects and Principles for Beginning Biologists by Frank G. Bottone, Jr. (Chicago, IL: Chicago Review Press, 2001)

Budding biologists get acquainted with the five kingdoms of life with 25 engaging projects using commonly found materials. As kids learn how to conduct experiments in carefully controlled environments, they determine which culture media is more effective at inhibiting bacteria growth, collect and compare night-flying and day-flying insects, and learn how to clone a mushroom. Plenty of background information is provided along with a glossary and websites to explore.

101 Kid-Friendly Plants: Fun Plants and Family Garden Projects by Cindy Krezel (Chicago, IL: Chicago Review Press, 2008)

Families looking to enrich their green thumbs while beautifying their homes will enjoy this comprehensive guide to indoor and outdoor gardening using non-toxic flowers, vegetables, trees, and houseplants. Sorted by type—plants from seed, bulbs, annuals, perennials, fruiting trees, and sensory plants—each plant is thoroughly explained and easy to identify using color photographs. Details such as the flora's preferred habit and why a particular plant is good for kids are included along with suggestions for use in the garden. Seventeen gardening projects illustrate a variety of creative and fun ways for children and parents to plant together, including butterfly gardens, herb pots, hanging baskets, rock gardens, and cutting gardens.

The Kids' Guide to Service Projects (2nd ed.) by Barbara A. Lewis (Minneapolis, MN: Free Spirit, 2009)

This new edition of Free Spirit's bestselling youth service guide includes a refreshed "Ten Steps to Successful Service Projects," plus hundreds of up-to-date ideas for projects—from simple to large scale. The book covers service projects for a wide variety of topics, including animals, crime fighting, the environment, hunger, politics and government, safety, seniors, and more. A special section gives step-by-step instructions for creating flyers, petitions, press releases, and more.

The Teen Guide to Global Action: How to Connect With Others (Near and Far) to Create Social Change by Barbara A. Lewis (Minneapolis, MN: Free Spirit, 2007)

This book includes real-life stories to inspire young readers, plus a rich and varied menu of opportunities for service, fast facts, hands-on activities, user-friendly tools, and up-to-date resources kids can use to put their own volunteer spirit into practice. Upbeat, practical, and highly motivating, this book has the power to rouse young readers everywhere.

It's Your World—If You Don't Like It, Change It: Activism for Teenagers by Mikki Halpin (New York, NY: Simon Pulse, 2004)

This book shows teens how to act on their beliefs and make a difference in the world. Information covered includes the basics of activism; activism projects and outreach ideas; how to be an activist at home, at school, and in the community; stories from teenagers who have taken on the world—and won; and resources including books, movies, and websites.

Unpuzzling Your Past (4th ed.) by Emily Anne Croom (Cincinnati, OH: F&W Publications, 2010)

Updated and revised, this edition presents all the tools family detectives need to research their past: interview formats, sample letters, worksheets, addresses, and more. "Things to Do Now" encourages readers to apply what they have learned, and a resource section, information on deciphering script, tips for finding out personality traits and physical features of distant relatives, and more round out this volume.

Word Wizardry: Make Words Magic by Margaret Kenda and William Kenda (Hauppage, NY: Barrons, 1999)

More than just clever word play, *Word Wizardry* invites youngsters to explore other countries via online newspapers, write radio news stories, analyze handwriting, upgrade a home page on the web, develop code, and much more. Creative activities using readily available materials help children uncover the origins of language and a variety of ways to use words and communicate well.

CSI Expert!: Forensic Science for Kids by Karen K. Schulz (Waco, TX: Prufrock Press, 2008)

Crime scene investigation is hotter than ever, and kids everywhere will love learning about how their favorite detectives use science to figure out unsolvable thefts, arsons, mysteries, and more. *CSI Expert!: Forensic Science for Kids* includes more than 25 in-depth activities on fingerprinting, evidence collection, bloodstain identification, forensic careers, ballistics, and much more.

Crime Scene Detective: Using Science and Critical Thinking to Solve Crimes by Karen K. Schulz (Waco, TX: Prufrock Press, 2006)

Watch the excitement ripple through your classroom as students use their intellect to find out who committed the "crime" at your school. Enliven your students as they practice critical thinking skills. Students are often taught skills such as the scientific method, scientific research, critical thinking, making observations, analyzing facts, and drawing conclusions in isolation. Studying forensic science allows students to practice these skills and see theories put into practice by using circumstances that model real-life events, meanwhile letting students explore a variety of career options.

Inventions, Inventors, and You by Dianne Draze (Waco, TX: Prufrock Press, 2008)

This combination of research and creativity training allows students to explore how our lives have been affected by inventions while they build their own creative skills. From a youngster's playful attempts to use objects in new ways, to the adult's efforts to solve everyday problems, we see the inventive mind analyzing at all times. If you're planning an invention convention, put this book on your must-have list!

Mystery Disease by Mark A. Bohland (Waco, TX: Prufrock Press, 2006)

A serious illness is sweeping through town. Why are people getting sick? What is the source of this disease? With this problem-based learning unit, students become public health workers as they track down the source of a mysterious illness. Working in teams to solve the real-world problem and present their findings, they experience genuine, higher order learning. Decisions they make affect the outcome of the simulation.

Mystery River: A Problem-Based Ecology Unit by Mark A. Bohland (Waco, TX: Prufrock Press, 2008)

This unit introduces students to a serious problem—the fictional town of Hopewell's prized freshwater mussel population is dying out, and the town's leading citizens cannot figure out why. Your students will take charge of the situation as they join a task force dedicated to solving the problem.

Mystery at Golden Ridge Farm: An Interdisciplinary Problem-Based Learning Unit by Theresa Van Praet (Waco, TX: Prufrock Press, 2014)

A local, community-supported agricultural farm has noted a mysterious lack of produce for a number of consecutive years. Unable to explain why or how the produce is disappearing, the farm owners ask the students of a local school for help. Students work in collaboration with the farm as they assume the role of detectives and investigate the problem from every angle.

101 Hands-On Science Experiments by Phil Parratore (Waco, TX: Prufrock Press, 2008)

A must-have science resource for teachers of gifted children in grades 4–7, this book presents 101 exciting demonstrations that will engage students in the science curriculum and make them eager for the next classroom experiment. Advanced science concepts covered in the challenging experiments include temperature, motion, chemical reactions, pressure, light and colors, and plant science.

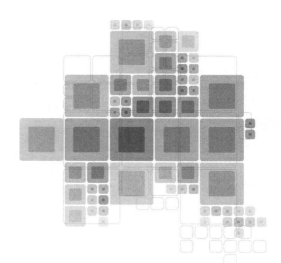

ABOUT THE AUTHORS

Joseph S. Renzulli is a longtime faculty member of the Department of Educational Psychology at The University of Connecticut and was selected by the university as one of its Distinguished Professors. He holds dual directorships at the Neag Center for Gifted Education and Talent Development and the federally funded National Research Center for the Gifted and Talented.

Marcia Gentry is the director of the Gifted Education Resource Institute and Professor of Educational Studies at Purdue University. Her research has focused on the use of cluster grouping and differentiation, the application of gifted education pedagogy to improve teaching and learning, student perceptions of school, and nontraditional services and underserved populations.

Sally M. Reis is the Vice Provost of Academic Affairs and a Board of Trustees Distinguished Professor at The University of Connecticut. She was a public school teacher for 15 years and worked with academically talented students on the elementary, junior high, and high school levels. She is a well-known scholar and has authored or coauthored more than 250 articles, books, book chapters, monographs, and technical reports.

INDEX

audiences, 14, 64–67
authentic methodology, 13, 118, 119, 159,
    how-to resources, 13, 30, 177–187

content escalation, 27, 28
crafts and hobbies, 42

data gathering, 77–80, 124–126
    instrument development, 78
Deductive Model, 5–7
Dewey, John, 5, 7, 9, 22
division of labor, 31, 32, 72

enrichment clusters
    defined, 17–20
    descriptions, 19, 33, 42, 54, 55, 67–69
    grouping, 25, 38, 100, 169–175
    guidelines for developing, 63
    research, 1–3, 7–10, 12–15, 17, 22, 23, 25,
        27–31, 38, 39, 41, 42, 62, 64, 65, 67, 69,
        70, 72, 76, 77, 79, 80, 82, 89, 125, 126,
        130–132, 135, 137, 151, 153, 154, 161,
        162, 163, 164, 169, 173, 177, 178, 181,
        182, 185, 186, 189
    teaching methods, 54, 155–157
    evaluation, *See* also program evaluation,
        124–126

facilitators, *See* staff development, 54, 55, 87,
    118
Facilitator Evaluation and Feedback Form, 139

high-end learning, 5, 9–12
    defined, 9–11

Inductive Model, 5–7, 20
interests, 2, 7, 9, 14–16, 18, 20, 23–25, 29, 32,
    34, 38–40, 42, 43, 47, 48, 50–52, 57, 62, 68,
    69, 72, 81, 96, 97, 100, 104, 105, 107, 109,
    115, 117, 120, 146, 148, 152, 153, 155, 156,
    158–160, 162, 167, 171

surveys, 39, 42, 78, 126, 136

If I Ran the School, vii, 38, 39, 42, 165
Inspiration, 25, 39, 40, 48, 63, 103, 105
Interest-A-Lyzers, 24

key questions, 63–66

leadership. *See* program leadership, 33

planning forms and documents, 105–113
Product Planning Guide, 112–113
program evaluation, 124–126
    forms, 54, 56, 58, 124–126
program implementation, 85, 119

real-world problem, 11, 12, 186
    defined, 12, 13, 14
registration, 55–58

scheduling, 33, 34, 43, 46, 48, 141
staff development, 34, 59, 85, 87, 96, 118
    locating facilitators, 48–53
    orientation, 54, 115, 118
state content standards, 20, 21
student-driven learning, 2–4, 14, 15, 33, 52, 54,
    61, 87
    defined, 2–4

wall chart, 40–42, 115, 117